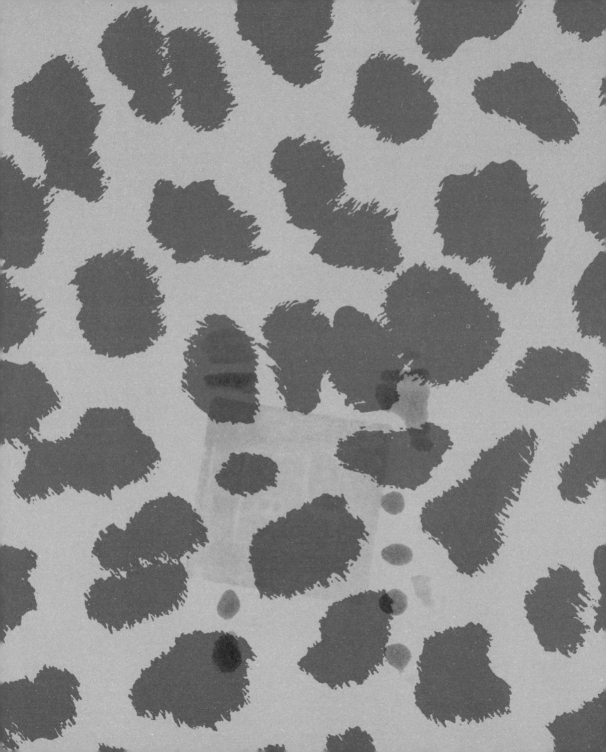

Designer Dogs

TAMMY GAGNE

Designer Dogs
Project Team
Editor: Heather Russell-Revesz
Copy Editor: Stephanie Fornino
Indexer:
Design concept: Leah Lococo Ltd., Stephanie Krautheim
Design layout: Angela Stanford

T.F.H. Publications
President/CEO: Glen S. Axelrod
Executive Vice President: Mark E. Johnson
Publisher: Christopher T. Reggio
Production Manager: Kathy Bontz

T.F.H. Publications, Inc.
One TFH Plaza
Third and Union Avenues
Neptune City, NJ 07753

*Discovery Communications, Inc. Book
Development Team:*
Marjorie Kaplan, President, Animal Planet Media
Carol LeBlanc, Vice President, Licensing
Elizabeth Bakacs, Vice President, Creative Services
Brigid Ferraro, Director, Licensing
Peggy Ang, Director, Animal Planet Marketing
Caitlin Erb, Licensing Specialist

08 09 10 11 12 1 3 5 7 9 8 6 4 2
Printed and bound in China

Library of Congress Cataloging-in-Publication Data
Gagne, Tammy.
  Designer dogs / Tammy Gagne.
     p. cm. – (Animal Planet pet care library)
  Includes index.
  ISBN 978-0-7938-3791-5 (alk. paper)
  1. Dogs. 2. Dog breeds. I. Animal Planet (Television network) II. Title.
SF427.G24 2007
636.7'1–dc22
                              2007022082

This book has been published with the intent to provide accurate and authoritative information in regard to the subject matter within. While every reasonable precaution has been taken in preparation of this book, the author and publisher expressly disclaim responsibility for any errors, omissions, or adverse effects arising from the use or application of the information contained herein. The techniques and suggestions are used at the reader's discretion and are not to be considered a substitute for veterinary care. If you suspect a medical problem consult your veterinarian.

The Leader in Responsible Animal Care for Over 50 Years!®

www.tfh.com

Table of **Contents**

Chapter 1

Why I Adore My

Designer Dog

The names of many designer dogs can elicit a giggle from even the most serious dog fancier. After all, it's hard to even say words like Goldendoodle and Puggle for the first time without smiling a bit. And Pekeapoo? It sounds more like a game than a dog, doesn't it? Not everything about these increasingly popular crossbred dogs is lighthearted, though. There is an astounding number of both fans and critics of these unique hybrids, and their reasons are as different as the designer dogs themselves.

Designer Dog or Mutt: What's the Difference?

Crossing two separate dog breeds (outcrossing) is hardly a novel concept. In fact, outcrosses have been made in nearly every modern-day breed—and often for admirable reasons. Crossbreeding Saint Bernards with Newfoundlands, for instance, virtually saved the former breed from extinction in the 1800s after an exorbitant number of Saints had perished performing their trademark rescue work. Many other breeds—the Basset Hound, the Poodle, and the Shih Tzu, just to name a few—have been outcrossed at some point in their history to hone the dogs' size, coloration, or coat texture. When looked at from a historical perspective, the word purebred might even be perceived as a relative term. Still, the American Kennel Club (AKC) does not recognize any of the designer dogs discussed in this text, making it impossible for them to be AKC registered or compete in the club's conformation shows.

Hybrid Vigor

We've all heard that mixed breeds can be some of the healthiest dogs in existence, and to some degree this is true. Without the persistent genetic health problems associated with purebred dogs, mutts are indeed less prone to countless afflictions, simply because they are not in demand like so many purebreds. It is essential to point out, however, that designer dogs are *not* mutts. Whereas a "Heinz-57" has numerous different breeds in his ancestry—and such a mix is often the result of an accidental encounter—a designer dog has two very carefully chosen parents. Also, a designer dog is typically the result of only two primary breeds. Like mongrels, though, a designer dog can be healthier than either of his parent breeds, especially if the parents are not predisposed to the same genetic illnesses. This benefit to designer dog breeding is referred to as hybrid vigor.

The Allergy Factor

Another common selling point for designer dogs is their reputation for being easy on the eyes—literally. Many poodle hybrids are said to pose fewer problems to allergy sufferers than purebreds. While numerous owners and breeders agree that this advantage is a legitimate one, a fair number conversely insist that there is no such thing as a truly nonallergenic dog. Harsher critics

Is That Really a Word?

A portmanteau is a word that is formed by fusing two existing words and combining their meanings right along with their letters. What do you get when you cross a Schnauzer and a Poodle? Why, a Schnoodle, of course! Don't look for this portmanteau in Webster's, though. As of yet, the only two designer dogs to make it into the dictionary are the Cockapoo and the Puggle.

Unlike the mixed breed (above), the Pekeapoo puppy on the right is the result of carefully chosen parents.

assert that many designer dog breeders use both the allergy factor and hybrid vigor as justification for charging inflated prices for their animals.

What's in a Name?

Some blame the stigma associated with hybrid dogs on the name itself. "I detest the term *designer dog*," one Labradoodle breeder confided to me, adding that she thinks it gives the practice of crossbreeding a superficial connotation. "I breed for the same qualities a reputable breeder of purebred dogs does—good health, reliable temperament, and consistent physical attributes."

A breeder of Cocker Spaniels had this to say on the debate: "Some of the crosses are adorable. I don't think there's anything wrong with breeding hybrids." She then clarified, "as long as

Designer Dog Spotlight

If you own a designer dog, you are in good company. A list of Puggle owners alone reads like a Who's Who of Hollywood. Uma Thurman, Jake Gyllenhaal, Julianne Moore, and James Gandolfini all own this popular designer hybrid. Think you have anything in common with Ashley Judd? You do if you own a Cockapoo—or two, as she does. Jessica Simpson has an adorable Maltipoo named Daisy. Famous Labradoodle fanciers Jeremy Irons and Tiger Woods make no secret of being designer dog owners, but perhaps the most famous Labradoodle to date is kept in a box—of the classic board game Monopoly, that is. A special edition of the game features a metal Labradoodle game piece in place of the traditional Scottish Terrier.

the breeders are using good judgment in selecting the parents and not making unrealistic promises to potential owners." Many purebred breeders aren't as open-minded. One even went so far as to say that designer dogs will never join the ranks of their purebred contemporaries in the registries of the AKC.

So are designer dogs destined to be permanently censured for their dual-breed pedigrees? I don't think so, but it may be a long time before purebred enthusiasts accept designer dogs as valid breeds in their own right. Some may always shun them. To many designer dog fanciers, this matters little. Some fear that once a particular designer dog is officially recognized, the dog's popularity will increase, and reckless breeders will rush to meet the demand at the expense of the puppies produced. If a designer dog were ever to earn recognition from the AKC, though, my money would be riding on either the Labradoodle or the Cockapoo, two of the oldest and most popular designer hybrids. There

are also a growing number of hybrid dog registries abounding throughout the world, including the American Canine Hybrid Club (ACHC), which acknowledges approximately 400 different types of designer dogs.

Designer Dog Breeding

Breeding designer dogs is a serious undertaking, far more complicated than merely pairing two purebred dogs and waiting for nature to take its course. Take the Labradoodle, for example. An educated breeder will start by selecting a healthy, attractive purebred Labrador Retriever and an equally worthy purebred Poodle, but the resulting litter is usually just the beginning. Often the next step is to take a dog from this first-generation Labradoodle litter—one who most closely matches the look for which the breeder is striving—and then breed him (or her) back to either a purebred Lab or Poodle. This practice of continuing to use purebreds in breeding may persist until the desired characteristics are achieved consistently. A breeder may produce several generations before breeding doodles to doodles, for example. Most of the puppies produced in early litters are sold as pet-quality dogs (those with inferior physical characteristics for breeding but excellent potential as family pets), with the stipulation that they must be spayed or neutered.

Puggles, on the other hand, are said to retain their finest qualities when produced directly from their parent purebreds, the Pug and the Beagle. Two Puggles typically produce little but erratic results in their litters. Still, breeders must use extreme scrutiny when selecting these dams and sires. The goal always should be to combine the very best of both breeds.

There are no guarantees that even two dogs of the same breed will produce a litter of pups that all match their American Kennel Club (AKC) standard, yet the AKC must register every dog if a breeder so chooses. Although he may never be blessed with the title of champion, a dog falling far short of his breed standard may even be used in breeding future generations of purebreds.

Breeders with a personal preference for a characteristic that lies in direct opposition to the standard may even work to consistently produce that quality in her litters. Like any purebred dog, a designer puppy's fate rests largely on his breeder's professional ethics.

To many fanciers, the deciding factor between designer dogs and purebreds is a bit of a conundrum. Although neither dog in fact possesses a completely pure heritage, the designer dog is prevented from being officially recognized as a breed of its own because he doesn't have a sufficient number of different breeds in his line. For a new breed to even be considered for inclusion in the AKC's list of 155 recognized breeds, it must

The American Canine Hybrid Club acknowledges about 400 designer dogs, like this Comfort Retriever (Golden Retriever-Cocker Spaniel cross).

have at least 4 different breeds contributing to its creation— and even then acceptance is only a possibility. With nearly 250 independent breeds that do fit this requirement still absent from the AKC list, designer dogs are sitting pretty at the end of a long line of potential inductees.

Oodles of Poodles

It is no coincidence that the names of so many designer dogs end in a *poo* or an *oodle*. The Poodle's nonshedding coat is a highly coveted trait among designer dog connoisseurs, but there are also other reasons that this purebred is such a popular designer dog foundation. Poodles are known for being among the smartest of all purebred dogs, and their temperaments frequently match their impressive intellect. Retrievers are also popular cross choices for these same reasons.

Many dog lovers are choosing designer dogs for the simple reason that owning one can be like having two dogs in one. Suppose you love the athleticism of a Golden Retriever, but you also fancy the curly coat of the Poodle. In a Goldendoodle, you just might find your

The Expert Knows

The ABCs of F1, F2, and F3

The pedigree of a designer dog can read a bit like an advanced algebra equation. Knowing some basic hybrid breeding terminology can make this seemingly complicated document a much less confusing piece of paperwork. An F1 Yorkipoo, for example, is a first-generation hybrid. This simply means that his parents were a purebred Yorkshire Terrier and purebred toy Poodle. An F1-B Yorkipoo is the result of breeding an F1 back to either a purebred Yorkshire Terrier or a purebred Poodle. An F2 Yorkipoo has two F1 parents. Like the F1 Yorkipoo, an F2 is exactly 50 percent Yorkshire Terrier and 50 percent Poodle. An F3 is a cross between two F2 Yorkipoos. In most cases, it is the F3 or later generation dogs who produce the greatest consistency in their litters.

ideal dog, a mix that seems like it was *designed* especially for you.

Schnoodles and Doodles and Pomchis, Oh My!

With hundreds of dog breed combinations available, it can be difficult to decide which hybrid is right for you. Perhaps you already know you'd like a poodle cross, but which one? Or maybe you adore spaniels, but can't decide between the Cockapoo and the Cavachon. The designer dogs described in this section are among the most popular crosses being bred today.

Cavachon

The Cavachon is a cross of the Cavalier King Charles Spaniel and the Bichon Frise. Like the Puggle, this designer dog possesses the best qualities when his parents are both purebreds. The Cavachon is known equally for his low- to nonshedding coat and his extremely kind nature. Cavachons are also intelligent, playful, and wonderful with children who treat them properly. Like the Labradoodle, quite possibly the Cavachon's polar opposite in size, this little dog loves the water and can be surprisingly active, despite his relatively low exercise requirements.

A Cavachon is a cross between a Cavalier King Charles Spaniel and a Bichon Frise.

Although Cavachons may weigh anywhere from 12 to 28 pounds (5 to 13 kg), most dogs fall around the midpoint of this rather wide range. Unlike the purebred Bichon Frise, who is almost entirely white, the Cavachon's coloring is more like the Cavalier's. This hybrid may be peach and white, peach, sable and white, black and tan, or tri-colored. Many Cavachons also sport the Cavalier's signature *thumbprint*, a spot on the forehead considered one of the most desirable physical characteristics of this purebred.

Although the coat type can vary from dog to dog, most Cavachons are soft and silky. Frequent brushing will be necessary if your dog's hair is kept long. Fortunately, this hybrid looks great in a short pet clip, but even this low-maintenance look requires at least a weekly brushing.

Cockapoo

The Cockapoo is a designer dog who has been around longer than the designer dog craze. This hybrid, which crosses the American Cocker Spaniel with a toy or miniature Poodle, has been bred since the 1960s here in the US, where it originated. When I was growing up, one of my neighbors had a beautiful cream-colored Cockapoo. At this time, my family owned a purebred miniature Poodle, and I remember noticing many similarities between the two dogs in both temperament and appearance.

Because Cockapoos have been bred for so long, it is now extremely common for breeders to breed one Cockapoo to another, although some lines are still being developed by breeding back to purebreds to perfect certain characteristics. While both parent breeds of this designer dog have a painstakingly coiffed appearance, the Cockapoo is said to resemble another product of my childhood: Benji. The coat is unclipped (although scissoring will be necessary to keep hair out of the eyes), the tail is undocked, and strangely enough, the dog's appeal is only enhanced by skipping these steps that are virtually mandatory for his purebred parents. The look is not unlike the infamous Farrah Fawcett hairdo of the '70s—long, tousled, and absolutely stunning.

All colors and combinations are considered acceptable, but kinky curls are not. The Cockapoo's nonshedding coat should instead be straight, wavy, or loosely curly. If your dog's long flowing locks are too much for your grooming schedule, you may opt to shorten them to prevent matting. One Cockapoo owner I know gives her dog a lighter haircut during the summer and allows him to grow out during the colder months of the year for added warmth.

Like Poodles, Cockapoos come in different sizes. A dog weighing less than 12 pounds (5 kg) is classified as a toy Cockapoo. Dogs falling between 13 and 18 pounds (6 and 8 kg) are labeled miniature. While the largest Poodle variety is called a standard, the largest Cockapoo—weighing more than 19 pounds (9 kg)—is identified as a maxi.

No matter what his size, a Cockapoo should have a sweet and patient nature. Like his ancestors, this designer dog is known for being intelligent, loyal, and friendly. Dispositions can vary among individuals, of course, but a calm and mellow disposition is the goal for any responsible breeder. This is more important than any other trait.

Goldendoodle

The origin of the Goldendoodle, a cross of the Golden Retriever and the Poodle, is a bit unclear. While many US breeders insist that the hybrid began in the states, a fair number of Australians claim this doodle to be their own achievement. Now popular in many other countries as well, Goldendoodles are bred for many of the same reasons that Labradoodles are. These smart and fun-loving dogs make excellent working animals, particularly

A Cockapoo is a cross between a Cocker Spaniel and a Poodle.

for people with frustrating allergies. It should be noted, however, that like any other designed dog, the coats of Goldendoodles can differ from one individual to another. Some dogs shed as much as Golden Retrievers, while others inherit the nonshedding coat of the Poodle.

There are currently no size classifications for the Goldendoodle, but most dogs are the product of pairing a Golden Retriever with a standard-sized Poodle. These pups may grow to between 20 and 24 inches (51 and 61 cm) and weigh from 45 to 75 pounds (20 to 34 kg), with males on the larger side. Occasionally, Goldendoodles are bred from miniature or toy Poodles; in these cases, artificial insemination is utilized, with the dam always being the Golden Retriever. The resulting dogs from these litters typically measure between 13 and 21 inches (33 and 53 cm) tall and weigh from 25 to 45 pounds (11 to 20 kg).

From this designer dog's name, one might logically expect him to be blonde or gold. It is the Poodle side of the pedigree, though, that actually determines an individual dog's coloring. Goldendoodles may be white, blonde, tan, café, chocolate, red, black, silver, parti, or phantom. One litter may even contain a variety of these drastically different colors.

Like the purebreds of their origin, Goldendoodles are extremely sociable and highly trainable. They are excellent swimmers and retain a strong retrieving instinct from their agile ancestors. Also like purebred Goldens, they are great with kids. This makes them ideal family pets.

Labradoodle

In the 1980s, an Australian dog breeder named Wally Conron crossed a Labrador Retriever with a Poodle in hopes of creating a guide dog for blind allergy sufferers.

A Goldendoodle is a cross between a Golden Retriever and a Poodle.

A Labradoodle is a cross between a Labrador Retriever and a Poodle.

for the Australian Labradoodle to one day gain official recognition from the AKC.

Labradoodles may be white, gold, brown, or black. Although early generations may develop a variety of coat textures, there are generally two types of coats for which most breeders strive: wool and fleece. Wool coats do not shed, while fleece coats sometimes do, making them a bit less desirable.

Probably the most carefully developed designer dog to date, the Labradoodle now has a strong following throughout the world. These dogs are highly trainable, and many late-generation offspring are indeed well tolerated by people with allergies.

You may hear the term Australian Labradoodle and wonder how this hybrid differs from ones without an outback heritage. Several other breeds—including several spaniel breeds, other types of retrievers, and terriers—have been utilized in the Australian Labradoodle's development. For this reason, breeders of the Australian Labradoodles emphasize that there is a considerable difference between their dogs and Lab–Poodle crosses originating more recently in other countries. It may even pave the way

A Labradoodle's size is primarily determined by the variety of the Poodles used in the lines. Dogs measuring between 14 and 17 inches (36 and 43 cm) tall and weighing no more than 30 pounds (14 kg) are classified as miniature Labradoodles; those falling between 18 and 21 inches (46 and 53 cm) in height and weighing between 35 and 48 pounds (16 and 22 kg) are considered medium; and dogs reaching heights of 21 inches (53 cm) or more are deemed standard-sized Labradoodles.

This designer dog adores water. Labradoodles are adept swimmers and also will readily join you for countless other physical activities. Be cautious about leaving them outdoors, though, because they are notorious diggers.

Maltipoo

A Maltipoo may be the result of breeding a purebred Maltese with a purebred toy Poodle, or his parents may be hybrids themselves. Another low-shedding designer dog, the Maltipoo has a soft and fluffy coat that comes in an array of colors. Lighter shades are most commonly seen, affording this petite canine an even more delicate appearance. Don't be fooled by his dainty facade, though. For a dog weighing only between 5 and 12 pounds (2 and 5 kg), the Maltipoo is surprisingly quick to defend his family or what he considers his territory, especially if he is startled by an intruder.

Although Maltipoos inherit their personality traits from both the Maltese and the Poodle, the former purebred appears to have slightly more

A Maltipoo is a cross between a Maltese and a Poodle.

FAMILY-FRIENDLY TIP

Go Meet Your Match!

Once you have assembled a list of designer dogs known for being good with children, the next step in finding the right puppy for your family is visiting with different breeders together. Watch how each dog responds to you and your family members, especially the younger ones—and look for your kids' reactions, too. Even if a particularly hybrid looks perfect on paper, what matters most is that you all feel comfortable with the pup you choose.

influence on the typical Maltipoo's temperament. This is not a dog to be left alone all day while the owner works. Maltipoos are extremely emotional beings and will often take out their frustrations on their owners' belongings to make their point.

Though certainly not the most common designer dog, the Maltipoo is growing in popularity. This is likely because of the hybrid's loving and giving nature. This designer dog is deeply empathetic, gravitating toward ill family members or others in need of a devoted companion. They are also known for being playful but gentle with children.

Pekeapoo

A cross of the purebred Pekingese and the toy Poodle, the Pekeapoo is as good-natured as his name sounds. Although this 9- to 20-pound (4- to 9-kg) dog enjoys lazing on the couch as much as a cat, he also revels in playtime and adores children. He is highly affectionate and intensely devoted to those he loves.

Because the Pekeapoo is still under development, this designer dog has very few well-defined characteristics. In general, there are three acceptable colors: white, gray, or cream, the most common color. Unless you fancy the dreadlock look, you may want to consider keeping your Pekeapoo's soft and cottony fur short because it has a strong tendency to mat. It *is* possible to keep the coat long, but this requires at least twice-daily brushings. A second

A Pekeapoo is a cross between a Pekingese and a Poodle.

reason to break out those clippers, though, is to minimize tear staining, a common problem for Pekeapoos. Even with a short haircut, your dog will still need to be brushed a minimum of every other day. A small amount of hair will come out in this process, but more importantly, this designer dog sheds very little dander, the main trigger for most allergies.

Pomchi

A hybrid of the Pomeranian and the Chihuahua, the Pomchi is primarily a lapdog. This toy-sized companion is an excellent choice for a mature adult or couple, but this is not the best pet for an extremely active person or a family with young children. The Pomchi typically bonds most intensely with one person, and the dog's favorite pastime quickly becomes spending time relaxing with that individual.

The Pomchi stands between 6 to 9 inches (15 to 23 cm) tall and usually weighs between 5 and 12 pounds (2 and 5 kg). Although owners must be careful not to step on or play too roughly with this delicate hybrid, the Pomchi enjoys playing as much as any dog. He will readily run around and chase small balls or squeak toys when provided with a safe open space and will only benefit from being able to do so. If you don't have a big backyard, it's not a problem for this designer dog. A Pomchi can easily get in a full workout in an apartment with an average-sized living room.

Although some Pomchis are fluffier than others, most hybrids of this variety sport a full coat of beautiful fur. You can easily see both the Pomeranian and the Chihuahua in this dog, although a breeder need not cross purebreds for a good-looking specimen. This dog is available in a wide range of solid colors, as well as parti-colored, merle, and sable varieties. Brushing is necessary to keep his striking mane looking good, but trimming is usually only necessary around the feet and bottom to maintain a neat appearance.

Puggle

The Puggle is one of the most popular canine hybrids of the 21st century. This designer dog actually originated more than 20 years ago when a man named Wallace Havens of Madison, Wisconsin, bred a purebred Pug to a purebred Beagle. Havens, now a supporter of many designer dogs, promoted the Puggle from the beginning, but the dog's biggest notoriety has come within just the last few years.

This small dog with a wrinkled muzzle and sad eyes typically weighs between 7 and 30 pounds (3 and 14 kg), measuring 10 to 15 inches (25 to 38 cm) at the shoulders. Most Puggles resemble the Pug, being fawn colored with a black mask, but some are solid black or multicolored. Because the Puggle does shed a small amount, he is not considered a hypoallergenic dog.

The Beagle ancestry affords the Puggle a larger and slightly longer body than a Pug. Like the Beagle, the Puggle also has adorably floppy ears and a longer nose—a likely benefit in view of

A Puggle is a cross between a Pug and a Beagle.

the health problems associated with the Pug's shorter snout. Generally the Puggle is indeed healthier than the Pug, but this designer dog may suffer from more health problems than a purebred Beagle.

Puggles have a reputation for being excellent pets for families with children. They are content to sit in a lap or jump up and play at moment's notice. This lively temperament can be a detriment for owners during training, however, because it can distract the dog from the task at hand. Like both parent breeds, the Puggle also has a tendency to be hyperactive.

Schnoodle

The Schnoodle, a cross of the Schnauzer and the Poodle, is said to be another nonallergenic member of the designer dog group. His fine fur grows much like human hair, making shedding much less of an issue but snarls a dogged problem if this hybrid isn't brushed at least weekly. The Schnoodle also needs regular trimming, but without a distinct haircut of his own, this dog may be a refreshing change for a creative groomer. If one prefers a detailed styling guide, however, it is safe to say that many Schnoodle 'dos resemble that of a terrier, a short pet-style clip with relatively long fur left on the dog's face. Colors include black, white, brown, gray, and apricot. Multi-colored dogs are also frequently seen.

Most Schnoodles are the result of pairing a purebred miniature or standard Schnauzer with a purebred miniature Poodle. Dogs from these litters typically weigh between 11 and 16 pounds (5 and 7 kg) as adults. When most people mention a Schnoodle, this is the dog to whom they are referring. If the Schnauzer parent is a very small one, a toy Poodle may be used instead of a miniature one, resulting in what is called a toy Schnoodle. Breeding giant Schauzers to standard Poodles is also done occasionally, but the giant Schnoodles from these litters, like the giant Schnauzer breed itself, are prone to many problematic characteristics—including an extremely demanding activity level, aggression toward other animals, and a tendency to be precariously overprotective of children.

More moderately sized Schnoodles are known for being devoted and intelligent companion animals. Keenly perceptive, they are said to be an ideal combination of the Poodle's sharp mind and the Schnauzer's desire to please his owner. Your Schnoodle may seem to know what you are going to do before even you are fully aware of it.

Yorkipoo

Like the Maltipoo, the Yorkipoo is a tiny poodle cross with a huge zest for life. Achieved by breeding a purebred Yorkshire Terrier with a purebred toy Poodle, this hybrid also shares many other characteristics with its Maltipoo cousin. For starters, this brave little canine is not as widely known as many of

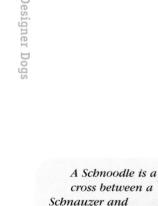

A Schnoodle is a cross between a Schnauzer and a Poodle.

When Is a Designer Dog Considered a Senior?

Larger dogs enter their golden years a bit earlier than smaller ones. A Labradoodle or Goldendoodle, for example, would be considered a senior pet when he reaches six years of age. Mid-sized designer dogs such as Puggles, Cockapoos, and Schnoodles generally aren't considered seniors until they are approximately seven years old. Some of the tiniest designer dogs—Maltipoos, Yorkipoos, Pekeapoos, Cavachons, and Pomchis—may reach the age of eight or nine before they start to show signs of their age.

proportioned dog. The smooth coat is silky and wavy and comes in a variety of colors. A common word associated with this designer dog is spunky. They are also very social. Not only do Yorkipoos enjoy the company of fellow Yorkipoos, but they also delight in romping with other kinds of dogs—and cats. They are said to be only okay with children, though.

When it comes to housetraining, the Yorkipoo tends to be a quicker learner than the purebred Yorkshire Terrier. Perhaps this is a result of the Poodle's notable trainability. They simply love learning.

A Yorkipoo is a cross between a Yorkshire Terrier and a Poodle.

the larger designer dogs. Additionally, a Yorkipoo may be the product of two purebred parents or two hybrids, although the former scenario is more common. Like so many designer dogs, the Yorkipoo's fur is also considered nonallergenic.

Standing approximately 7 to 12 inches (18 to 30 cm) tall and weighing from 4 to 15 pounds (2 to 7 kg), the Yorkipoo is a small but well-

Chug

Hybrid name	Cross
Affenpoo	Affenpinscher x Poodle
Alusky	Alaskan Malamute x Siberian Husky
Bagle Hound	Basset Hound x Beagle
Baskimo	American Eskimo x Basset Hound
Beaglier	Beagle x Cavalier King Charles
Bichon-A-Ranian	Bichon Frise x Pomeranian
Bocker	Beagle x Cocker Spaniel
Brat	American Rat Terrier x Boston Terrier
Brottweiler	Brussels Griffon x Rottweiler
Buggs	Boston Terrier x Pug
Bullmatian	Bulldog x Dalmatian
Cadoodle	Collie x Poodle
Carkie	Cairn Terrier x Yorkshire Terrier
Cav-A-Malt	Cavalier King Charles x Maltese
Cheeks	Chihuahua x Pekingese
Chiweenie	Chihuahua x Dachshund
Chorkie	Chihuahua x Yorkshire Terrier
Chug	Chihuahua x Pug
Cock-A-Tzu	Cocker Spaniel x Shih Tzu
Comfort Retriever	Cocker Spaniel x Golden Retriever
Doxle	Beagle x Dachshund
English Mastweiler	Mastiff x Rottweiler
Faux Frenchbo Bulldog	Boston Terrier x French Bulldog
Foodle	Poodle x Toy Fox Terrier
Foxy Russell	Jack Russell Terrier x Toy Fox Terrier
Goberian	Golden Retriever x Siberian Husky
Havamalt	Havanese x Maltese
Jack-A-Bee	Beagle x Jack Russell Terrier
Malkie	Maltese x Yorkshire Terrier

Bagle Hound

Designer Name?

hybrids the American Canine

Faux
Frenchbo
Bulldog

Hybrid name	Cross
Miniature Schnoxie	Dachshund x Miniature Schnauzer
Muggin	Miniature Pinscher x Pug
Paperanian	Papillon x Pomeranian
Peke-A-Pap	Papillon x Pekingese
Pineranian	Miniature Pinscher x Pomeranian
Pinny-Poo	Miniature Pinscher x Poodle
Poochon	Bichon Frise x Poodle
Poolky	Poodle x Silky Terrier
Poshies	Pomeranian x Shetland Sheepdog
Pugland	Pug x Westie
Pugottie	Pug x Scottish Terrier
Pug-Zu	Pug x Shih Tzu
Saint Berdoodle	Poodle x Saint Bernard
Schweenie	Dachshund x Shih Tzu
Scoodle	Poodle x Scottish Terrier
Sharp Eagle	Beagle x Chinese Shar Pei
Sheltidoodle	Poodle x Shetland Sheepdog
Shocker	Cocker Spaniel x Shiba Inu
Skypoo	Poodle x Skye Terrier
Sniffon	Brussels Griffon x Miniature Schnauzer
Snorkie	Miniature Schnauzer x Yorkie
Swheat-N-Poo	Poodle x Soft Coated Wheaton
Taco Terrier	Chihuahua x Toy Fox Terrier
Wauzer	Miniature Schnauzer x Westie
Wee-Poo	Poodle x Westie
Weimardoodle	Poodle x Weimaraner
Welshund	Dachshund x Welsh Terrier
Woodle	Poodle x Welsh Terrier
Yorkipoo	Poodle x Yorkie

Chiweenie

Taco Terrier

Chapter 2

The Stuff of

Everyday Life

There are a few things that every dog owner needs. Thankfully, these items aren't numerous—and most are fairly inexpensive—but they all help to keep a dog safe and content. Once you have collected these basics, you can then decide which of the more indulgent choices may be helpful to you and your individual dog.

Bed

Although I have two dogs, there is only one dog bed in my home. At the moment it is filled with virtually every toy my dogs own. You may find that your dog appreciates a bed of his own more than my two do, especially if you don't allow him to sleep on your bed with you. I have to confess that mine have both slept with my husband and me since the day they each arrived in our home.

If your designer dog is a small one, though, allowing him to share your bed can actually be dangerous. A fall from this height could seriously injure or even kill him. If your dog must sleep on your bed, consider investing in a set of *pet steps*. This portable staircase can only protect your dog if he uses them faithfully, however.

The best way to train your dog to use a bed of his own is by introducing it early. Puppies may chew or soil this item, though, so you may want to begin with a less expensive bed and upgrade to a more luxurious one as these juvenile behaviors become a thing of the past. An even more practical option is to use an old blanket during those first few weeks.

If you cannot get your dog to stay in his bed (or on his blanket), consider letting his crate serve as his sleeping quarters. You won't have to worry about accidental falls or overnight housetraining mishaps, and he will not be able to jump up on your bed once you are asleep. Once this habit begins, it is mighty hard to break.

Collar and Leash

Choosing the right collar size and leash material for your designer dog is essential.

Collar

Collars for your designer dog are available in nylon and leather. Nylon

Your puppy will love a comfy bed of his own.

collars are the best option because they are extremely versatile, and many offer breakaway technology. This important feature helps to protect a pet if his collar ever becomes caught on another object.

To measure your dog for a collar, use measuring tape to determine the size of his neck. Place the tape around his neck, and make sure that you are able to fit two fingers comfortably between your pet's neck and the tape. If your designer dog is a tiny one, leaving enough space for just one finger is preferable.

Leash

Every dog needs a leash, even if he spends most of his outdoor time in a fenced yard. Most municipalities legally require dogs to be leashed whenever they visit a public place. Even if your dog only uses a leash when he visits his veterinarian, he should be taught how to walk on a lead while he is young. If not, you will likely be faced with a frustrating battle when it comes time to attach this necessary tether to him as an adult. He also may pull you along and even chew at the lead itself.

Although larger dogs like Labradoodles can tolerate chain leashes better than smaller ones can, I recommend avoiding metal leads altogether. Chain should never be used on toy designer dogs such as Pomchis or Maltipoos, because it is much too

The Expert Knows

No Time to Lose!

One of the most important things you can do for your dog is to establish a routine for him. Although this may seem daunting when your new pup is housetraining and needs to be taken outdoors every two hours, you will soon thank yourself for remaining consistent. Dogs eating at the same time each day will also eliminate at predictable times. During the training phase, you may find that keeping track of your dog's successes and failures with a chart is helpful. This can alert you to any glitches in your routine and enable you to make the necessary adjustments. Remember to make exercise an integral part of your routine. If you find that your dog is having a tough time discerning a leisurely walk from elimination time, consider using two different leashes for these very different activities. Your dog will soon associate each task with its corresponding leash.

heavy for their delicate necks. The best material for conventional leashes is nylon. It is durable, washable, and available in a complete array of attractive colors and designs, most with matching collars.

Many owners (and dogs) enjoy the benefits of extendable leads. These long leashes that extend and retract to suit a variety of situations are literally like having several leashes in one. They are especially useful for owners who live in the suburbs, where a walk can mean navigating through a busy intersection at one point and running on grassy knolls just minutes later. Mimicking the freedom of being off-

lead, an extendable lead also can come in handy when teaching your dog to come when called, because you can let him venture out a bit while still retaining control over his compliance of the command.

Harness

Similar to a leash but worn around the chest instead of the neck, a harness is often a better option for a notorious wriggler who has discovered how to escape a collar. When measuring your dog for a harness, place the tape around your dog's chest, just behind his front legs. While both large and small dogs can wear harnesses, they are particularly useful for smaller designer dogs because they eliminate the risk of an owner inadvertently pulling too hard at their more fragile necks.

Crate

Providing dogs with a place to eat and sleep no matter where their owners travel with them, a crate also offers dogs something more personal: a private sanctuary. My own dogs readily head to their crates whenever I give them an especially delectable treat, and I often find them lolling inside their kennels during nap times. I initially had my qualms about crates; to me they seemed similar to cages for wild animals, certainly not something for beloved pets. To my pleasant

surprise, I found not only that crates are highly preferable to the spots my dogs sought out when left to their own devices (primarily under desks, where the dangers of power cords and outlets lurked), but also that my canine companions seem to truly appreciate this space of their own.

Types of Crates

I use plastic crates because they are easy to assemble and disassemble for cleaning. Most airlines require this rigid-style kennel for flying, so if you plan to fly with your dog, buying a plastic crate now will save you the expense and hassle of purchasing a second crate later. I also like the added privacy a plastic crate provides. Although the dog can easily see out of any side through built-in vents, the interior is shaded, which makes it an ideal setting for rest and relaxation.

A wire kennel, on the other hand, offers a gregarious dog an excellent means of feeling like he is part of the household happenings. If bright light is an issue when sleeping, a blanket or towel can be placed over the kennel. Wire is also a better option if your dog is a chewer.

Most crates come with a set of plastic dishes that attach to the cage door. Although these may be fine for travel, I recommend investing in an additional set of metal dishes if you plan to routinely feed your dog in his crate. Again, plastic is extremely vulnerable to the whims of a chewer. Plus, using plastic dishes can cause a condition called plastic dish nasal dermatitis. Caused by an antioxidant in the plastic, this disease can bring about irritation and swelling. More visibly, it can result in a loss of skin pigmentation on the dog's nose and lips.

Size

Because crates are also extremely useful for housetraining, it is particularly important that you select a kennel that

What Size Crate Does My Designer Dog Need?

Recommended Crate Size	Designer Dog
Extra small: approximately 18 to 22 inches (46 to 56 cm) long	Maltipoo; Pomchi; Yorkipoo
Small: approximately 24 inches (61 cm) long	Cavachon; Cockapoo, toy; Pekeapoo; Puggle; Schnoodle
Medium: approximately 30 inches (76 cm) long	Cockapoo, miniature; Labradoodle, miniature
Intermediate: approximately 36 inches (91 cm) long	Cockapoo, maxi; Goldendoodle
Large: approximately 42 inches (107 cm) long	Labradoodle, medium
Extra large: approximately 48 inches (122 cm) long	Labradoodle, standard

This Goldendoodle loves lounging on the bed, but a crate can give him a safe, secure place of his own.

is the proper size for your pet. Think of your Goldendoodle like Goldilocks—his crate shouldn't be too big or too small, but *just right*. If the interior is too spacious, he will likely use one end as a makeshift bathroom. If it is too small, he will feel cramped inside it. Ideally, your dog should be able to stand up and turn around easily within his crate, but he shouldn't be able to walk from one end to the other. If your puppy is presently too small for an adult-sized crate, there are even models with removable partitions, making them adjustable within a certain size range.

Liner

Whether you select a plastic or wire crate, you will also need a liner. This custom-fit cushion will help to keep your dog comfortable. Most pet supply stores offer a wide assortment of crate liners, ranging from simple fleece versions to velvety microfiber filled with orthopedic foam. Make sure that the one you choose is machine washable, and consider purchasing two instead of just one so that you always have a clean one ready on laundry day. Of course, you can always use a folded blanket or towel in lieu of a liner. This may be useful during travel because it can serve multiple purposes, but you may find refolding it constantly to be a bit exasperating on a day-to-day basis at home.

Exercise Pen (X-Pen)

Typically made up of eight foldable sides, an x-pen is a freestanding structure that provides similar benefits as a safety gate. Unlike a gate, however, an x-pen can be placed wherever you want to use it. If there is enough room, you can set it up in your kitchen or living room. If you want your pup to get some fresh air, you can assemble it in your backyard. These canine playpens can be especially useful to owners who do not have fenced yards.

Food and Water Bowls

Picking out dishes for your dog was once a simple task, but now that the choices include inverted cone-shaped bowls that keep long ears out of water and fountains with built-in water purification systems, shopping for canine dinnerware can seem much more complicated. It doesn't have to be overwhelming, though. Every dog should have at least one set of stainless steel bowls. (I always keep two sets so that there is a clean set waiting when the dirty ones head into the dishwasher.) Stainless steel dishes are strong, easy to clean, and typically nest within each other for easy storage.

Unlike stainless steel dishes, ceramic bowls can sometimes be dangerous to your pet's health. Ceramics intended for human use must follow strict safety guidelines, but there are currently no requirements for pet dishes in terms of lead content. Therefore, when going the ceramic route, only buy table-quality items. Although ceramic bowls can be found in fun colors and patterns that match your home's décor, they are also extremely susceptible to breakage—and aren't always dishwasher safe. I learned this the hard way once when I retrieved one from my dishwasher and found that it had lost most of its design in the washing process.

Plastic dishes are inexpensive, shatterproof, and like ceramic, come in a variety of pleasing colors. In

SENIOR DOG TIP

The Second Time Around

Many people mistakenly assume that adopting an older dog means dealing with problem behaviors. Oftentimes dogs' original owners have experienced major life changes such as divorce or financial hardship, making it impossible for them to care for their pets. Older dogs are frequently far less demanding than puppies. They are usually already housetrained, and they typically have considerably less energy than their younger counterparts. Even a well-adjusted adult animal will need time to acclimate to a new setting, though.

You can make this easier on your adopted dog by being patient with him during his transition into your home. It may take days; it may take weeks; it may even take months. Most importantly, spend as much time with him as possible during this period. The closer you bond, the fewer problems you will have.

addition to the threat posed by plastic nasal dermatitis, however, plastic is highly vulnerable to

FAMILY-FRIENDLY TIP

Child Care

There is no better way to teach a child how to properly treat an animal than showing her as you care for a shared pet. Young people also have a lot to offer dogs in the way of companionship, play, and even simple forms of care. It is vital, however, that any tasks a child is allowed to perform are age appropriate. While a toddler can certainly be included in the housetraining process, for instance, she won't be able to hold your dog's leash when you walk him. A more practical task for a two-year-old might be praising your pet when he eliminates in the proper spot during housetraining.

Even older children should never be relied upon to care for animals on their own. Teenagers, though mature enough to handle a variety of tasks, may not remember to perform them as dependably as an adult. Making certain tasks your teen's responsibility is fine, but always double-check to make sure that these jobs have indeed been performed as needed.

chewing. Of these three most popular materials, plastic is my third choice for these reasons.

Gate/Baby Gate

Sometimes called a baby gate, a safety gate is especially useful for owners who prefer not to use a crate. After puppy-proofing a small room in your home, using a gate will help to keep your dog safe when you cannot watch him. Some models pressure-mount, making it possible for you to use them in any doorway. Others attach with permanent hardware and offer the ease of swing-style doors.

Be sure to place the gate low enough to prevent your dog from slipping underneath, or worse, getting caught between the gate and the floor. Also, avoid accordion-style gates because they present a strangulation risk. Gates made of hard plastic, metal, or wood are available at most pet supply stores, but you also can find them in many department stores in either the pet or baby sections.

Even if you do use a crate, I recommend investing in at least one gate. My dog Damon learned to climb stairs at just eight weeks of age, but he didn't master coming back down until he was nearly five months old. Instead he would sit in our upstairs hallway and cry until someone came to retrieve him. As soon as I realized how often I was providing this shuttle service, I began placing a gate at the foot of the stairs to thwart the initial trip.

Every Dog Has His Daycare

If you work long hours, you may consider enrolling your dog in doggie daycare. This practical service can provide your pet with attention, exercise, and socialization when you cannot. Always request a tour of the daycare and ask any questions you may have before committing to a program. The facilities should be clean and well organized, and larger dogs should be kept separate from smaller ones. There also should be criteria for admission, including temperament evaluation and proof of vaccinations.

If your dog isn't the social type, a better option may be a professional dog walker or pet sitter. This person will come to your home and take your dog outdoors to stretch his legs and relieve himself. You will need to trust this person with a key to your home, as well as with your precious pet, so be selective when interviewing candidates for the job. Check references, and heed any warning signs (either your own or your dog's) that a specific person isn't the right one.

Grooming Supplies

The most important grooming tool any dog owner needs is a brush. Although the style may differ depending on your dog's coat type, all dogs need regular brushing. For longer-haired designer dogs, the most obvious goal is to prevent mats and tangles, but both long- and short-haired dogs also must be brushed to remove dirt and other debris from their coats. For a short-haired designer dog like the Puggle, a soft-bristled brush will do the job wonderfully. A slicker brush, however, is a better choice for a dog with long or curly hair, such as the Cockapoo. A metal flea comb is also a smart idea for any designer dog. I use a comb to test my brushing. If it flows through my dog's fur without a hitch, I know I've done a thorough job.

The next thing you will need is a set of nail clippers. Keeping your dog's nails trimmed to a reasonable length keeps him looking good and feeling comfortable. Overgrown nails hurt, and they can easily become caught on rugs or clothing. They also can cause your dog to injure himself or others. If you can hear your dog's toenails on the floor, a nail trim is already overdue. There are three basic types of nail clippers: pliers-style, guillotine-style, and scissors-style. Which type is best is purely a matter of personal preference; however, many owners of large dogs find scissors-style clippers to be a bit more difficult to use on their pets.

Finally, you will need to purchase a few disposable items to meet your dog's grooming needs. A quality shampoo and conditioner top this list. You also will need ear cleanser and canine toothpaste. A toothbrush is optional if you don't mind restocking your dog's grooming bag with gauze

Make sure that your designer dog is properly identified—this Pekeapoo is much safer with his ID tags.

If your dog is ever stolen, however, you will need proof of ownership in a form that cannot be removed. By far the most popular method of permanent pet identification is microchipping. Even a tattoo, the most popular ID method in decades past, can be altered by a resourceful thief. Less conspicuous than a tattoo, a microchip is inserted under a dog's skin in a procedure as quick and painless as a vaccination. The tiny chip, approximately the size of a grain of rice, then remains with your dog wherever he goes, affording him an identification number that can quickly be read by a veterinarian or rescue worker with a handheld scanner.

A microchip can only help to reunite you with your dog if you are reachable. You must register with the parent company—and just as importantly, inform them if and when your contact information changes. Another smart safety precaution is to take regular photographs of your pet. Particularly if your dog has any features that distinguish him from other members of his designer breed combination, a simple snapshot can help you prove that you are indeed his true owner. In addition, this visual reference can be used in your search for him.

from time to time. I find that my own dogs tolerate this impromptu brushing medium much better than the brushes designed specifically for pets.

Identification, Please

In addition to obtaining a dog license from your local municipality, you also should consider attaching a personalized identification tag to his collar. This inexpensive item can be purchased at most pet supply stores and can be engraved on the spot with your pet's name as well as your own name, address, and phone number. If your pet is ever lost, his ID tag can serve as an instant ticket home to you.

Toys

While a Pekeapoo and a Goldendoodle may favor different kinds of toys, all dogs enjoy play. Like children, dogs

Do You Have Your Dog's Number?

need playthings. Similar to the way our kids utilize toys, dogs often prefer interactive toys that can be used in games with their family members. Balls are a popular choice, but the selection hardly ends there. There are squeak toys, stuffed toys, scented toys, and even edible toys. How do you know which is best for your pet? Experiment! You may not even think that your dog is a toy connoisseur until you find just the right one.

Not only do toys stimulate a dog's mind and help fend off boredom, they also provide an excellent opportunity for exercise. If you have a roomy backyard or frequently visit dog parks with your pet, consider purchasing a ball with an attached strap or a throwing wand. A device like this can enable you to propel the ball up to 100 feet (30 m) or more, turning playtime into a fun and challenging workout for your dog. If your space is more limited or your designer dog is a smaller one, you may prefer to use a more conventional ball and roll it instead of tossing it.

When your dog spends time alone, you may want to offer him a toy such as a nylon bone or a treat-dispensing game to pass this time. Chew toys can help your dog release tension and simultaneously prevent problem behaviors such as inappropriate chewing and even aggression. A toy that contains a hollow section for edible substances such as peanut butter can be used for this purpose or as an incentive for crate training.

Finally, never underestimate the power of a play fest. The toys themselves mean far less than an owner's willingness to make time for play. A ball is only an inert object unless there is someone to throw it. Select toys that appeal to you, as well as your dog—and set aside time each day to use them with your pet.

Does your Maltipoo not want to share? Make sure that you have enough toys to go around!

Chapter 3

Good Eating

Eating is one of the most enjoyable pleasures available to all animals. Whenever my dogs see me head to the kitchen, tails start wagging as we play an impromptu game of follow the leader from the food pantry to the counter. Like me, my dogs relish the lovely tastes that food offers, but I also delight in knowing that feeding my dogs healthy food also means providing them with the nutrients their bodies need to keep them looking and feeling their best.

To Their Health!

Like people, dogs need protein for the growth and repair of body tissue. Dogs' bodies also utilize carbohydrates in a similar way as people to provide them with long-term energy. Dogs need a higher amount of fat in their diets than humans do, though, due to their more efficient metabolism. They also need certain vitamins (primarily A, D, E, B-complex, and K) and minerals (such as calcium). Finally, they need water to help to transport all these nutrients throughout their bodies.

It is important that your dog's vitamins and other nutrients are offered in the proper amounts and ratios. Some vitamins are toxic when given in excess. Likewise, too much fat can lead to unnecessary weight gain and heart disease. The best way for your dog to get the right balance of all his nutrients is from his food.

Commercial Foods

Buying dog food once meant deciding if you wanted the small bag or the huge feed-bag size. Now the choices are more about what is inside the bag—or the can, or the roll. Instead of picking up our pets' food at the grocery store, we make a special trip to the pet supply store and look for ingredients that best match our dogs' dietary needs. If you own a smaller designer dog like a Yorkipoo, a bite-sized formula is a sensible choice. A Labradoodle, on the other hand, has a lower requirement for calcium and phosphorous, so a large-breed formula that provides just the right amounts of

SENIOR DOG TIP

Antioxidants and Anti-Aging

Did you know that your dog's food can actually help him age better? Antioxidants such as vitamin E and beta-carotene help to reduce free radical particles that lead to body tissue damage in older pets. These antioxidants also strengthen the immune system and should be a regular part of a senior dog's diet. If your dog's kibble lacks these important nutrients, you can offer them in the form of fruits, vegetables, and grains—such as mangoes, carrots, broccoli, red and yellow peppers, and wheat germ.

these nutrients is preferable in his case. It is not only your designer dog's breed combination that helps to distinguish his ideal diet, though. Perhaps your Cockapoo is involved in agility; a high-energy food may be best for him. Or maybe your Puggle has gained a little extra weight, in which case a weight-reduction formula is indicated.

Dry Food

Dry food is the most popular choice for owners purchasing a commercial food.

This makes sense, as the advantages are numerous. Dry kibble can be stored in bulk without waste, and it is easy to feed because it requires virtually no preparation. Owners can feed their dogs a certain amount at a specific time, or they can leave a full bowl available throughout the day.

Canned Food

Take a walk through your local pet supply store, and you will see that canned food is also a very popular choice among dog owners. This type of food has its advantages. Like dry dog food, canned or wet food can easily be purchased in advance without worry of spoilage. Allowing wet food to sit in your dog's bowl for long periods of time is not a safe option for your pet, though. Leftovers should always be refrigerated until your dog's next meal and consumed within a few days.

Brush your dog's teeth frequently if he is on a canned regimen. Feeding crunchy treats will definitely help, but wet food has a way of jumping on the fast track to morphing into calculus, the clinical term for tartar. Oftentimes this is not even visible until it has already solidified. Canned food also can mean looser stools. This doesn't affect your dog's health, but it can be rather unpleasant for the person in charge of yard cleanup.

Semi-Moist Food

While dry and wet foods always seem to have their die-hard supporters who prefer one kind to the other, semi-moist regimens tend to have more critics than enthusiasts. Although your dog may be more than willing to finish every morsel of this attractively packaged meal (many are sculpted into burger shapes), most semi-moist foods contain excessive amounts of sugar. Not only is this bad for your designer dog's teeth, but it is also especially dangerous for dogs with diabetes or weight problems (a risk factor for the disease).

If your dog likes the flavor of a semi-moist food, a healthy alternative to the mainstream options is something called a dog food roll. Packaged similar to salamis, these foods offer a compromise—pleasant taste *and* good nutrition. As with any type of food, though, you must check the label to make sure that the brand is nutritionally sound.

Noncommercial Options

Buying a prepackaged food is not a dog owner's only option. More and more people are discovering that one of the best ways to provide their pets with the healthy foods their bodies need is by preparing their dogs' meals

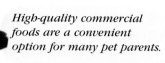

High-quality commercial foods are a convenient option for many pet parents.

Meeting Your Designer Dog's Changing Nutritional Needs

Puppies Up to Four Months	Puppies Between Four Months and One Year	Adult Dogs (1 to 6 years)	Senior Dogs (approx. 6 to 9 years and older)
Choose a quality food made specifically for your designer dog's size. Younger puppies need more protein than older dogs. They also need to eat more frequently. Feed your new puppy three times a day, dividing the total amount of food given among these meals. Offer water with each meal, but while you are housetraining, be sure to remove it about an hour or two before bedtime.	Once your puppy reaches four months of age, you can eliminate his midday meal. Somewhere between the ages of 4 and 12 months, your small designer dog should be swapped over to an adult food. Although larger designer dogs aren't ready for this transition until they are between one and two years old, smaller dogs reach their adult size well before this time, thus requiring less protein. As soon as housetraining is complete, you also can begin to offer water at all times.	Most adult dogs should eat two meals per day. Again, look for diets specially formulated for your designer dog's size. Not only will these regimens contain the specific combination of nutrients your dog needs, but the food also will be sized appropriately. You can offer variety in the form of healthy snacks like raw vegetables. Just be sure to watch your dog's weight, because metabolism slows with age. Superfluous pounds (kg) will only be harder to lose as your dog approaches his senior years.	The senior designer dog's diet is perhaps the most individualized of all age groups. If your dog has any health concerns, your veterinarian may recommend feeding a specialty diet. If your dog is in good health, he may need a change of some other sort to renew his interest in eating. Wet food or home cooking can often help with this. Because a dog's nutritional needs (and metabolism) change once again at this time, changing to a food made specifically for seniors is a good idea. You also may want to discontinue feeding harder foods if your dog's teeth are in poor shape or if he is missing teeth.

personally. Although this may sound like a complicated process, in many cases it is no more time consuming than preparing a meal for the rest of your family. In most cases, your designer dog can even eat the same foods as the other members of the household, with just a few exceptions.

Home-Cooked Diet

When most people think of preparing food, cooking is what comes to mind. Fresh steamed vegetables, lean meats, and even a small amount of fruits and grains are all healthy choices for any designer dog. Just like people, your dog shouldn't be getting too many refined sugars, fried foods, or other empty calories, though. Instead, offer vegetables such as broccoli, sweet potatoes, and leafy greens and chicken with whole-grain pasta or rice. Avoid dairy because most dogs are lactose intolerant, and never give a dog chocolate or onions, which are highly toxic to all canines.

The down side to home cooking is that it leaves your dog's teeth more susceptible to plaque and tartar, so you must make regular brushing a priority if you go this route. Also, it is especially important that your dog receives all the vitamins and minerals his body needs. The best way to ensure this is by discussing your menus with your veterinarian. She will be able to help you fill in any gaps that could cause a deficiency in your pet's diet.

The best part about home

Read Up!

Before I select a new food for my family, I always check the label for a breakdown of the ingredients. If there is too much fat or sugar in a particular item, I usually return it to the shelf and keep looking. The process of choosing nutritional food and treats for my dogs is very similar. Like people food packages, dog food bags and cans must include a guaranteed analysis of the amount of various nutrients, such as protein, fat, carbohydrates, and fiber. This labeling also lists any preservatives used in the manufacturing process. If the food you are considering doesn't meet your nutritional standards, continue studying those labels until you find one that does.

39

cooking is that it does not have to be an all-or-nothing undertaking. If you are finding it difficult to provide your dog with the right amount of protein (or other nutrients), you may decide to supplement your home-cooking regimen with a small amount of dry kibble. Likewise, even if you feed a commercial food, you can add some home-cooked fare into your dog's diet. Just be sure to adjust the amount of his prepackaged intake so that he isn't getting too many calories.

Raw Diet

The concept of feeding a dog a diet comprised strictly of raw foods may at first seem rather primitive. The basis for this style of feeding that has

Good Eating

Is It Okay to Give My Dog Milk?

Few dog owners know that most dogs tend to be lactose intolerant. This means that they lack the enzyme beta lactamase, which allows the digestive system to break down the kind of sugar contained in milk.

Dogs who lack this enzyme end up with a lot of undigested sugar in their intestinal tract, which creates a wonderful breeding environment for bacteria. When a lot of bacteria grow in the intestinal tract, they can irritate the stomach and intestine and cause vomiting and diarrhea. These are the same problems that occur in lactose-intolerant people.

That being said, while many dogs are lactose intolerant, some are not. Some dogs love the taste of milk and other dairy products and won't have any stomach or intestinal problems when they get some as a treat.

The bottom line is that it may be okay to give your dog a small amount of milk if it doesn't cause him any vomiting, diarrhea, or other discomfort. Check with your veterinarian first to be sure that it won't cause your pooch any health problems or interfere with his diet.

Courtesy of the American Animal Hospital Association and Healthypet.com

become extremely popular in recent years, however, makes a lot of sense. Simply put, raw foods retain many of their innate health-enhancing benefits that cooking eradicates. Sometimes referred to by its acronym, the BARF diet (short for *bones and raw food*) inspires immediate images of blood-red meat and bones, and this certainly is part of the regimen. When used properly, however, one sees that meat is just one element in a very carefully designed and balanced diet. Other raw foods included in this plan are eggs, poultry, fish, fruit, and vegetables.

Many breeders and veterinarians recommend the BARF diet. Just as the advantages of this diet are numerous, though, so are the liabilities—as evidenced by the comparable number of canine health professionals who strongly discourage the practice of feeding raw food. Small dogs in particular are at considerable risk of suffering from broken teeth or intestinal injuries from bone fragments, but dogs of all sizes can experience these unfortunate injuries. A dog eating raw meat also may come in contact with such dangerous bacteria as salmonella and E. coli.

If you think that feeding raw food is worth the risk, do thorough research before transitioning your dog to an exclusively raw plan. As with home cooking, balance is key with BARF. If you don't do your homework, you can miss all the benefits that this regimen should provide—or worse, put your dog's health at risk due to a particular nutritional component that has been overlooked.

Supplements

Does your designer dog need a vitamin supplement? The best way to provide your dog with the vitamins his body needs is by selecting foods that are rich in these nutrients. If your dog has a medical condition, though, he may need more of a particular vitamin or mineral than he can realistically get from the food he eats. If your dog is arthritic, for example, you may find that adding glucosamine and chondroitin to his food can help to ease the pain of his stiff joints—and without the side effects of an anti-inflammatory medication. A good friend of mine swears by a popular flower essence solution that is said to bolster the immune systems of both sick and healthy pets. She uses this any time one of her dogs experiences a physical problem or increased stress due to other reasons. It is vitally important, however, that you check with your dog's veterinarian before offering your pet a new supplement of any kind. Numerous factors should be considered before determining which (if any) supplements are right for your dog. His entire diet, medical history, and other supplements or medications he is taking must be considered.

Free Feeding Versus Scheduled Feeding

Should you make food available to your designer dog at all times (free feeding), or is it better to feed him on a schedule? There is no correct answer for everyone. What works well for you and your dog may be the exact opposite of the option I choose for my canine duo. If you are keeping your dog's dish full and he isn't overeating, there may be no need to change him from his free-feeding regimen to a schedule. If he is gorging himself, though, or if you are having trouble keeping track of how much food he is consuming, a more precise feeding routine may be beneficial.

Eating too little also can be a concern with free feeding because loss of appetite is a common warning sign of illness, and it can easily be overlooked on a free-feeding plan.

Make plenty of fresh water available for your designer dog.

Even in healthy pets, having food available constantly can create a general disinterest in eating. Whether the number is high or low (or just right), your dog's weight is an excellent indicator if free feeding is working for your pet.

I recommend beginning with a routine. If your dog starts off this way, he can usually be transitioned to free feeding with few (if any) problems if you decide that this is the better choice. Changing a free-fed dog over to a schedule, however, can be a grueling task.

Obesity

Overweight dogs face an increased risk of countless conditions, including arthritis, cardiovascular problems, diabetes, poor muscle tone, and joint and ligament strain. Pets packing extra pounds (kg) also have a lower tolerance for heat, and it can be dangerous for them to be anesthetized if they need surgery. The best way to prevent all of these problems from developing is to make good nutrition and regular exercise a part of your pet's daily routine.

Like people, pets gain weight when they eat foods that are too high in calories, fat, or sugar. Feeding healthy food is a great first step, but portions must also be monitored. Your dog's weight will increase just as quickly if the extra fat and calories are coming from his dry food instead of table food. The same amount of dog biscuits and other treats can contain twice the calories of kibble, so limit these

Unless recommended by a vet, puppies (like this Labradoodle) should not need supplements.

to a reasonable frequency, and reduce the amount of your dog's other food when you do indulge him. Also, it is important not to rely on food as your sole method of treating your pet. Long walks and extra play sessions can make your dog just as happy as that cookie.

I have found that keeping my dogs fit has also helped me eat and exercise more regularly. On days when I would normally shy away from venturing outside because it's cold or rainy, my dogs remind me that their walks are non-negotiable. And while chopping carrots for their snack time, I realize that these veggies are also a better choice for me than my chocolate stash.

Good Manners, Please!

Can a dog really learn table manners? Yes! All it takes is a little training. For example, if your Schnoodle is licking his bowl clean within minutes of its hitting the floor, slow him down by swapping to hand feeding for a while. As your dog becomes accustomed to this more gradual pace of one piece of kibble at a time, his scarfing will become a habit of the past.

Even a persistent beggar can be transformed into a more polite pooch when you refuse to give in to the pressures of whining and barking during your own meals. If your Puggle continues to beseech you when you ignore his efforts, remove him from the room while you eat. Offer him the opportunity to act appropriately the next day (and the next), and escort him to his crate or another room each time he does not comply. Sharing with a well-behaved dog is fine, but you should never present an edible treat directly from the table to your pet. Instead, place food into your dog's dish at your kitchen counter. This will help to discourage him from petitioning you for his portion before you are ready.

Chapter 4

Looking Good

It was the first thing that attracted you to your dog: his looks. Even if your dog's appearance is now second or third on the long list of things you love about him, it is essential that you keep him looking good. Simple grooming tasks such as brushing and nail trimming help your dog feel comfortable and remain healthy. In fact, one of the best ways for you to show your dog how much you love him is by keeping up with his grooming needs.

Time Well Spent

Even if you send your dog to a professional groomer for more time-consuming jobs such as bathing and clipping, you will need to perform at least a few grooming tasks at home. Daily or weekly jobs such as brushing your dog's coat and cleaning his teeth are not only vital to his physical health, but they also offer a wonderful opportunity for you to deepen your relationship with your pet. Begin each grooming session with a relaxing massage, and follow up with a fun treat like an edible reward or a brisk walk. By making grooming enjoyable, you gain your pet's trust, so you can both look forward to this special and productive time spent together.

Coat and Skin Care

Every designer dog needs his coat and skin looked after—from the short coat of the Puggle to the curly coats of the Poodle and Bichon crosses and every coat in between.

Must-Have Supplies

You can pick up your designer dog's necessary grooming tools at any pet retailer.

Brush

With the exception of the Puggle, all the designer dogs covered in this book should have a properly sized slicker brush. Having a much shorter and smoother coat, the Puggle needs a soft-bristled brush instead. If your dog's coat needs trimming—like the Cockapoo's does—you also will need a set of clippers if you plan to cut his hair yourself. I highly recommend cordless versions because they allow owners to perform quick trims no matter where they are.

Coat and Skin Care Products

When selecting a shampoo and conditioner for your designer dog, a variety of factors must be considered. Is your dog's skin dry? If so, select a moisturizing shampoo and conditioner or products containing oatmeal, an effective ingredient for fighting itching and dryness. If your Cavachon's silky hair has a tendency to snarl, use a small amount of detangler before brushing or a detangling conditioner after shampooing. Even your dog's coloring may play a role in which hair

Grooming makes your dog look and feel better—just look at the before and after of this adorable Pekeapoo!

products you choose. To keep your white dog looking clean and bright, use a shampoo made especially for lighter-colored animals. Likewise, there are products made specifically for darker-colored pets.

Brushing

When I mention caring for your dog's coat, what task immediately springs to mind? Bathing, right? Bathing is indeed an integral part of proper coat care, but an even more important one is regular brushing. Brushing a dog not only removes tangles, but it also helps to remove dirt and other debris from his hair and spreads natural oils throughout his coat. Because most dogs spend some time each day self-grooming, routine brushing also can help to reduce the number of toxic substances your dog ingests— such as lawn chemicals, household cleaning agents, and harmful bacteria.

The best part about brushing is that it feels good. Even a dog who has not been brushed regularly in the past can be trained to tolerate the task for this simple reason. Another advantage to this essential grooming step is that it requires very little instruction. Virtually anyone willing to spend just a little time and effort can effectively brush any designer dog. So try to make time for this important task at least once a week, preferably daily.

Short Hair or Fur

If your dog has short hair, brushing is an even more straightforward job. With a soft-bristled brush, start at your dog's head and move toward his tail and down each leg as you gently push down on the brush as you move it across your pet's body. It is important that you reach the skin because merely running the brush over the fur's surface will not strip away the dead hair and dander. Be careful not to bear down too hard, though, as this can cause skin irritation.

Curly or Long Hair

If your dog has long or curly hair, a slicker brush will work best to remove any minor mats or tangles. Brushing frequently also helps to prevent knots from forming. Follow the same strategy as for a short-haired dog, but follow up by using a metal comb to make sure that you haven't missed any spots. Speaking of which, don't forget to brush your dog's belly and underarms, common areas for pesky snarls.

SENIOR DOG TIP

Grooming the Older Dog: Not the Same Old Story!

As your dog gets older, you must adjust his grooming routine to meet his changing needs. He will still need the same tasks performed, but you probably won't be able to approach them the same way you did when he was a more agile adult. For example, if your dog develops any benign lumps or bumps (a common side effect of aging), you will need to use a bit more care when brushing him to avoid hurting these sensitive areas. If he suffers from arthritis, it is especially important that you dry his fur completely before allowing him outside after a bath.

The biggest change you are likely to notice is the additional time most grooming tasks will take. If your canine senior citizen finds it difficult to stand for a complete nail trim, for instance, you may need to spread the task over several days, working on just a single foot at a time. What matters most is that you remain committed to these important jobs. Doing so will help to keep your dog looking—and feeling—his best.

Bathing

The most common advice for bathing a dog used to be this: Do it as infrequently as possible. Because the chemistry of a dog's hair and skin differs so dramatically from a human's, many people mistakenly assumed that cleaning was somehow less necessary in the canine species. While your own hair has a pH level of between 4.5 and 5.5, your dog's coat and skin do fall much higher on the pH scale—approximately a 7. This does not mean, however, that he doesn't get dirty! It simply means that you need to follow two basic rules whether you choose to bathe your dog as often as once a week or as infrequently as once every month or two. (The longer your dog's hair, the more frequently he will need bathing.)

The two rules for bathing your designer dog are:

1. You must purchase a quality canine shampoo (never use a human product).

2. You need to rinse him thoroughly after each use.

Proper rinsing is in fact the most important step in effective dog washing. If your dog's skin is dry or itchy after bathing, this common oversight is most likely the culprit. If your dog's hair tends to be on the dry side, use a moisturizing shampoo and follow up by conditioning, again using a canine product.

Where to Bathe

If yours is a smaller designer dog, such as a Maltipoo or a Pomchi, you may find that your kitchen sink is the most convenient place for bathing. Just be sure that you never leave your dog unattended. A fall from a counter could seriously injure your pet. Larger dogs—from Cockapoos to Labradoodles—will be most easily bathed in a conventional bathtub. Whichever spot you choose, though, always use a nonskid mat to prevent your pet from slipping.

Before You Begin

Begin by brushing your pet thoroughly and gathering all the necessary bathing supplies: your dog's shampoo and conditioner, at least two big and absorbent towels, a facecloth, a handful of cotton balls, and a bottle of mineral oil. I always take my dogs for a potty break before bathing them, and I turn the thermostat up a little before running the water during colder months. The time to do all of these things is *before* the bath, so take your time to ensure that you don't forget anything.

Bathing Your Designer Dog

First, place a cotton ball in each of your dog's ears. Then, use the sink sprayer or shower attachment to wet your dog's fur thoroughly. The water should be moderately warm—test it on your own hand first. Next, dispense a small amount of shampoo into your palm and begin rubbing your hands together to create a mild lather. Because dog shampoos are formulated differently than human cleansers, you may notice that your pet's shampoo isn't quite as sudsy as your own.

Beginning with the outside of your dog's ears, rub his body gently with your soaped hands down his neck, over his back, and to his tail and buttocks. Don't forget his belly and legs, but skip the face. You will wash this area

Some designer dogs' coats, like this Pekeapoo's, need to be trimmed with clippers.

afterward with water alone. Once you have rinsed your dog completely (I usually rinse mine twice), you can then apply the conditioner. Follow the bottle's directions to see how long the product should be left on, and then repeat the rinsing process.

Drying

After towel-drying your pet, you may then use a blow dryer or allow your dog to air-dry if that suits his coat style. Curly dogs tend to be the best candidates for air drying, since even straight-haired dogs can end up on the wavy side if left to dry on their own. No matter which route you choose, make a point of brushing your dog during drying time to avoid mats and rid your pet of any stray hairs that he has shed during bathing.

Dental Care

Few things can affect your dog's well-being on such a broad spectrum as his dental care. In addition to keeping his breath fresh and his teeth looking whiter, brushing your dog's teeth regularly also helps to prevent disease and illness. Bacteria from dental infections can infiltrate the bloodstream, placing your dog's heart, kidneys, and other

The Expert Knows

Go Over Your Dog With a Fine-Tooth Comb!

I have always enjoyed grooming my own dogs. I am no professional, but what I lack in technique I make up for in spirit during this fun time spent with my precious pets. I know well, though, that there is a more serious side to grooming. In addition to keeping him looking good, grooming helps to keep a dog healthy. It could even save his life. I discovered this one afternoon when I found what turned out to be a mast cell tumor on my dog, Jonathan. I was accustomed to checking Johnny for any new lumps or bumps, because he was getting older and certainly had his fair share. I always had my veterinarian check these growths, and most were thankfully benign. This tumor, though, was cancerous. Because I caught it early, my vet was able to remove it, and I was blessed with considerable more time with my best friend.

organs at an increased risk for countless health problems. If your dog's teeth are already laden with calculus, professional cleaning will be necessary. Ideally, though, you want to prevent this substance commonly called tartar from forming in the first place. The easiest way to do this? Routine brushing.

Supplies

Similar to shampoo, canine toothpaste differs dramatically from products made for human use. Unlike people, dogs cannot spit toothpaste out after brushing is finished, so it is imperative that you use a brand made specifically for dogs. Many of these are formulated to appeal to the canine palate, and more importantly, they won't make your dog sick.

Although a toothbrush may be helpful, it is not necessary—especially if your dog balks at the idea of allowing this foreign object into his mouth. A small square of wet gauze wrapped around your index finger can be a very efficient means of cleansing.

The first time you brush your dog's teeth, you may want to use just the gauze and plain water. The next time, try adding some toothpaste. A slow but steady approach will help your dog see toothbrushing as just another part of his day. He may even enjoy it.

How to Brush Your Dog's Teeth

Start each toothbrushing session by finding a quiet spot for the task. You may discover that your Pomchi feels most comfortable positioned on your lap, or you and your Goldendoodle may both prefer sitting side by side on the floor. Whatever your dog's size, the latter option is preferable if your dog flinches once you insert the brush or your finger into his mouth.

Working in an oval pattern, gently begin brushing at a 45-degree angle, directing the brush toward the tartar-prone areas where the teeth meet the gums. Be sure to reach the spaces between the teeth, too. Working on three to four teeth at a time, brush around each set of teeth

Make sure to rinse all of the shampoo out of your dog's coat.

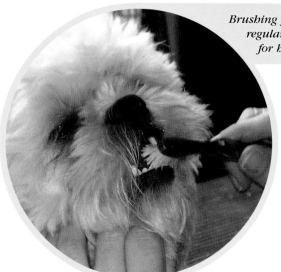

Brushing your dog's teeth regularly is important for his health.

approximately ten times, then move on to the next set. The first time you brush, you may only be able to clean your dog's top teeth—or maybe even just the front ones. Don't be discouraged; be dogged. Initially, you may need to revisit the task several times before you are able to finish the job.

Most importantly, don't stop because your dog fusses or wiggles. Instead, continue brushing for a short period, and always praise him for complying. Depending on his tolerance level, you may be able to continue the task a little longer. It is generally a good idea to end on a positive note, though.

Gradually increase the total number of teeth that are cleaned. A reasonable long-term goal is to accomplish two complete brushing sessions each week. Daily sessions are even better! I like to follow up brushing my own dogs' teeth by taking them for their morning walk

as soon as we finish. This affords them a fun reward and also helps to integrate the task into our daily routine.

Ear Care

After you have washed your dog's face, grab your mineral oil and remaining cotton balls to clean his ears. You may use ear cleaning solution available in most pet supply stores, but avoid products containing alcohol because these can irritate the skin. Begin by applying the oil to a cotton ball or squirting a small amount of cleaning solution into each of your dog's ears. If he shakes his head in response to this, don't worry. He will just be helping to loosen any dirt or excess wax. Next, using another cotton ball, gently wipe the inside of the ear. Repeat the wiping process until the cotton comes out mostly clean. (A tiny amount of wax is healthy, so don't expect it to look pristine.)

Although bath time is an ideal time to clean your dog's ears, be sure that this isn't the only time you perform this important task. Certainly, you may take advantage of the convenient opportunity that bathing presents, but strive to clean your dog's ears at least once a week. If you find it more difficult to get your dog to stand still when not in the bathtub, utilize the power of edible rewards. Offer one treat before the cleaning and another for each ear that is cleaned. I do this myself, and I have found that even though my dogs do not enjoy having their ears cleaned, they will line up immediately when they see me grab the cookies and cotton.

Eye Care

Good eye care is perhaps the easiest of all grooming tasks. The most important step: vigilance. Because so many designer dogs are susceptible to eye problems, it is essential that owners check their dogs' eyes regularly for signs of a problem. These include redness, excessive tearing or discharge, and obvious discomfort.

In addition to inspecting your dog's eyes, you also should be cleaning them routinely. Simply wipe the area around your dog's eyes gently with a soft washcloth dampened with plain water. Frequency will depend on the individual dog.

If you notice any signs of a problem, schedule an appointment with your veterinarian right away. Your vet will probably be able to treat your pet personally. If not, she can refer you to a veterinary ophthalmologist. A great preventive measure for many common eye problems is a routine visit

You can use mineral oil or an ear cleanser to clean your designer dog's ears.

to this specialist, so you may even want to ask for that referral before a problem arises. You also can help to prevent injury to your pet's eyes by keeping him away from items that pose particular risk, such as sharp furniture corners indoors or pointed vegetation outdoors.

Nail Care

No matter how large or small your designer dog is, his nails need to be trimmed regularly. It may be easier to see the nails on a short-haired designer dog, but even dogs whose fluffy feet camouflage overgrown nails can suffer from painful breaks or catch their nails on carpeting or clothing—or their own fur. Once you can hear your pet's nails when he walks across the floor, they are already overdue for trimming.

Although it can be a bit intimidating at first, owners can learn to cut their dogs nails themselves. The most important thing to remember is that trimming just a little bit of the nail more frequently is highly preferable to cutting off a large amount at any one time. By staying on top of this task, you will actually be lessening the risk of injuring your dog, for the more frequently the nail is cut, the more the quick (also called the

Be careful not to cut the quick when cutting your dog's nails.

nail bed) recedes. This is the pink area that bleeds if accidentally snipped.

How to Trim Your Designer Dog's Nails

Place your dog in standing position, holding his foot firmly and pressing gently on the pad to extend the nail. It is easier to see the quick on nails that are light in color, but unfortunately, individual dogs frequently have a combination of light- and dark-colored nails—sometimes even on the same foot. Using your clippers, snip off just the hook-like end of the nail on a 45-degree angle. Especially if you cannot discern the quick, err on the side of caution.

Continue this method until all the nails on the foot have been trimmed. For a puppy, it may take several days to finish all four feet, but the more often you trim, the more he will get

used to having this important job done. Touching your dog's feet at other times also will help to get him used to having his feet handled—a huge hurdle in the tolerance factor, so gently massage his paws as often as possible while he's young. Giving in to wiggling or whining by postponing the task will only teach your dog that these tactics work, so be persistent.

What if You Cut the Quick?

If you do the trimming yourself, chances are that you will accidentally cut the quick at least once. When this happens, remain calm and apply direct pressure to the area for 10 to 15 minutes with a sterile towel soaked in cold water. If the bleeding persists, you may use styptic powder (or pencil) to speed clotting. Other items that may be substituted include a soft bar of soap, cornstarch, or a wet tea bag. Finally, if you seem to be cutting the quick more often than not, consider leaving the job to a professional. Your dog will easily forgive an occasional mishap, but repeated injuries may result in a fear of nail trimming or a dangerous infection.

Professional Grooming

You may have a designer dog that needs intensive grooming, or you may find yourself without the time to properly care for your dog's coat. The answer is to find a professional groomer who will fulfill your grooming needs while treating your dog with the same amount of care and respect as you do. Choosing a groomer is a lot like selecting a daycare provider. You will want to ask many questions and carefully inspect the facilities before making your decision.

Where to Find a Grooomer

Although you can easily find a dog groomer by simply thumbing through your local phonebook, a better place to start is your breeder, veterinarian, or a friend who also owns a designer dog like yours. Recommendations from these trusted individuals are invaluable, and prevent you from having to start your search based on such superficial information as which business has the best ad. Another good resource for new dog owners seeking a groomer is the National Dog Groomers Association of America.

Bear in mind that no government agency regulates or licenses pet groomers. Although many groomers are registered or certified by their individual training schools or other organizations, it is still extremely important to interview a potential groomer and tour the facilities before leaving your designer dog there.

Initial questions may pertain to costs, hours of operation, and other general policies. If you think the business may be able to meet your needs, ask for references and follow up by contacting them. You should also contact the Better Business Bureau to find out if any complaints have been filed against the company.

FAMILY-FRIENDLY TIP

Grooming With Kid Gloves

When I was a little girl, brushing my family's Poodle was my job—or so I thought. I am now quite certain that my mother followed up on my earnest attempts to ensure that our dog wasn't being neglected due to my inexperience. This was a great strategy on my mom's behalf. I even employ it today with my own son. The older he gets, the more I can teach him about grooming. And the more he performs these tasks, the less follow-up work I must do. By assigning grooming tasks with these subdued checks and balances, you can build your child's confidence along with his budding abilities.

Looking Good

Chapter 5

Feeling Good

What have you done for your dog's health lately? Likely more than you think. Good canine health includes taking your dog to the vet regularly, making sure that he gets all necessary vaccinations, and watching him for signs of illness. It also includes feeding him nutritious food, helping him get regular exercise, and keeping him clean and well groomed. Even spending time with your dog affects his health— his mental health, that is. Yes, managing your dog's health is an expansive undertaking, but it also can be an enormously gratifying one. Just seeing your dog happy and healthy is well worth the effort.

Finding a Vet

The time to find a veterinarian is *before* your dog needs one. Ideally, you should select a vet before you choose your puppy because taking him for an initial checkup should top your to-do list once you bring him home. Many pet shops even stipulate that owners must take their dogs for a preliminary veterinary exam within a certain number of days from the sale for the store's health guarantee to remain valid. Perhaps you already have a vet you trust. If so, you are very lucky. Locating someone with the proper credentials to care for your dog's health is easy, but finding someone you feel comfortable entrusting with the care of your beloved canine companion is a much more thoughtful undertaking. Fortunately, there are many worthy veterinarians ready to assume this important job. Knowing how to identify these important caregivers is fundamental to your dog's health and your own peace of mind.

Take a Tour

You can learn a lot from telephoning a particular veterinary office or perusing its website, but nothing

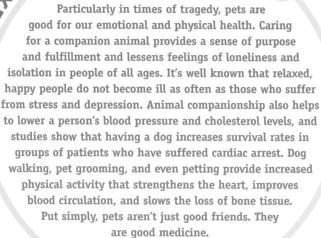

The Expert Knows

To Our Health!

Particularly in times of tragedy, pets are good for our emotional and physical health. Caring for a companion animal provides a sense of purpose and fulfillment and lessens feelings of loneliness and isolation in people of all ages. It's well known that relaxed, happy people do not become ill as often as those who suffer from stress and depression. Animal companionship also helps to lower a person's blood pressure and cholesterol levels, and studies show that having a dog increases survival rates in groups of patients who have suffered cardiac arrest. Dog walking, pet grooming, and even petting provide increased physical activity that strengthens the heart, improves blood circulation, and slows the loss of bone tissue. Put simply, pets aren't just good friends. They are good medicine.

Courtesy of the Humane Society of the United States

will yield as much information as taking a personal tour of the facility. Scheduling such a visit can serve as a forum for any questions you have, but equally important, it also provides you with an excellent opportunity to see for yourself how the vet interacts with both the staff and the animals. A happy staff is usually a sign of a positive working environment, but there is no better endorsement than your dog's. If he doesn't like a specific vet, look for other signs that this might not be the best person for the job. Animals have a keen intuition about people, especially undesirable ones.

In addition to the staff's rapport with you and your dog, there are other issues to consider when selecting a veterinary hospital. Are the facilities clean and well organized? Is someone available after business hours to monitor pets recovering from surgery? Will your dog always see the same doctor? Do they offer emergency services? (If not, add finding an emergency facility to that to-do list.) You may wish to ask if the hospital performs dentistry and lab work or if they have an in-house pharmacy that stocks commonly needed medications.

And don't forget to ask if referrals are made in situations that surpass the doctor's skills, such as orthopedics or alternative treatments.

Finally, don't forget to be an equal partner in your dog's health care. This means showing up on time for your dog's appointments, bringing along any necessary samples, and heeding your vet's advice.

Annual Vet Visit

Once your dog has completed his initial round of necessary vaccinations, you should only need to bring him to the vet once a year for a routine checkup. During this visit, your dog will be weighed and have his temperature taken, typically by one of the hospital's veterinary technicians, while she asks you general questions about your dog's health. This is a great opportunity to mention any concerns you have so that the tech can jot them down in your dog's chart along with his vital statistics. Your vet will then review this information when she enters the room a few minutes later.

The Exam

Your veterinarian will thoroughly examine your dog, checking his eyes, ears, and teeth; heart and lungs; and joints and kneecaps. It also may be time for certain vaccinations to be updated.

It's important to find a vet both you and your dog are comfortable with—this Goldendoodle's found a friend for life.

FAMILY-FRIENDLY TIP

Should I Bring My Child Along to the Vet?

Absolutely! I recently visited a website that listed practical activities for youth organizations. One idea was bringing the kids for a group visit to a veterinary hospital and having them follow up by giving a report on what they learn. I thought this was a great idea. Learning about the proper care of animals lays an ideal foundation for future pet owners, but it can be particularly useful for those youngsters who already share their homes with companion animals. Kids should be involved in as many aspects of your dog's care as they can based on their ages and individual maturity levels. Health care certainly tops this list. In addition to educating young people about the importance of bringing the family dog for routine exams and checking him regularly for signs of illness, by including your children in visits to your veterinarian, you also show them that important tasks such as temperature taking and necessary immunizations are quick and relatively painless. This can make their own trips to the doctor much less stressful for them.

Never be afraid to ask questions. One of the most important objectives of a responsible veterinarian is to educate clients so that they can help to keep their pets in the best possible health. By asking questions and doing your part, you make your vet's job easier.

In addition to helping you care for your dog's health, your veterinarian is an outstanding resource for information about training. If you are facing any behavior problems, mention them! Once a physical cause can be ruled out, your vet can then provide you with practical suggestions for reversing the situation. If the problem is a serious one, your vet can recommend a professional trainer or animal behaviorist.

Don't Rush!

Your dog's yearly veterinary exam won't take long, but don't rush through

These Labradoodle puppies will need to visit the vet for their first checkup and vaccinations.

61

it. If you are like most pet owners, your life is probably very busy. If you skip the question-and-answer portion of the visit or find yourself thinking about your next appointment instead of listening carefully as your vet talks to you, your dog's health could likely suffer. Avoid scheduling routine appointments during busy parts of your day or week so that you can be fully present once there, and make a list of any questions you may have ahead of time so that you won't forget them.

Whatever you do, don't skip a wellness exam. Although your dog may appear to be in perfect health, the best way to keep him that way is by consistently making—and showing up for—those routine appointments.

Vaccinations

Vaccinations have come under extreme scrutiny in recent years for triggering illnesses such as autoimmune diseases and other serious afflictions. Ongoing research and client-vet discussions about the side effects of vaccines have helped to bring veterinary medicine to a new, more interactive level of care. Like parents who are concerned for their children's safety, pet owners want to make sure that the shots their animals are receiving aren't harmful to their long-term health. Unlike children, however, our pets face the additional dangers associated with being vaccinated over and over for the same diseases. For this reason, many veterinarians are suggesting a more conservative approach to the vaccination process, based on individual risk assessment. All vaccinations carry certain side effects, but whether the need for vaccinating outweighs the risks these side effects pose depends on both the dangers

of the disease and an individual dog's particular lifestyle.

Optional Shots

Leptospirosis is an organism ingested through the urine passed by infected animals. If your dog is paper-trained or has an enclosed pen to which he is taken to relieve himself, his chance of coming in contact with infected urine is small. Because a higher risk of side effects—including anaphylaxis—is associated with leptospirosis-containing vaccines, vaccinating wouldn't be prudent in this case. If, however, you live in an area where both your dog and a plethora of wildlife share a backyard, you may want to consider the lepto shot. Remember, the animals need not occupy the space simultaneously for a high risk to be present. As we encroach upon their space, more and more wild animals frequent rural (and even suburban) neighborhoods at night while families and their pets are sleeping.

Combo Shots

Parvovirus, unlike lepto, is such a deadly disease that the risks of its side effects pale in comparison to the dangers of the disease. The parvo vaccine is included in a popular combination shot recommended by most veterinarians. The shot includes the vaccine that also protects your dog against distemper, another serious viral disease that is contagious, incurable, and often fatal. The most important thing to remember about combo shots is that one of these should never be administered at the same time as any other vaccination. Although most combinations are considered safe when given by themselves, whenever giving shots, the best guideline is the fewer the better. Receiving too many shots at one time can lead to any number of unpleasant side effects, including autoimmune diseases and even death.

Rabies

Another way that veterinarians have begun to minimize the risks of certain vaccines is by administering them less frequently. The rabies shot, for example, is now only required by law every three years in most of the United States, as opposed to annually or bi-annually, which was the standard schedule just a few years ago. The timetable may even be lengthened again in the future as more research is conducted on long-term immunity.

Educate Yourself

While the subject of vaccinations can be a scary one, the answer is not to skip vaccinations altogether, especially in the case of vaccines that are legally mandatory, like rabies, or those that legitimately need boosters, such as parvo. By and large, vaccinations protect our precious pets from a number of menacing diseases, many of which can be transmitted to other

The health of many designer dogs, like this Goldendoodle puppy, can benefit from hybrid vigor.

animals or humans. Even those that aren't communicable or zoonotic (transferable to people) can be ruthless. Lyme disease is one such illness. Unlike ticks of other varieties, the deer tick (the carrier of Lyme disease) is so small that most owners can easily overlook it even on a smooth-coated animal. Moreover, once the pinhead-sized tick is discovered, it is often too late—the disease can be transmitted to a healthy dog in just a day or two. Left undiscovered, it can be lethal.

Remember, your veterinarian is not the enemy. Most vets are pet owners just like you and me; they want what's best for the dogs, too. This is why many of them support changing the laws to best match our pets' veterinary needs. The best approach is selective vaccination based on education, so talk to your vet about the best choices for your dog.

Illnesses That Commonly Affect Designer Dogs

Every breed or breed combination is prone to at least a few illnesses. This does not mean, however, that every dog will be afflicted. By learning about the diseases for which your dog is at an increased risk, you can use vigilance to head off a problem before it can escalate into a more serious situation. You might even be able to avoid it altogether.

One advantage to owning a crossbred dog is that the risk of many diseases common in one of the parent breeds can be lessened if the other parent breed is not predisposed to the same illnesses. This is known as heterosis or hybrid vigor. One might wonder, though, if there is

SENIOR DOG TIP

Improving the Senior Status Quo

As your dog enters his senior years, his health care becomes even more important because early detection is crucial for the successful treatment of so many illnesses. Although a few changes may be necessary, the best way to ensure your older dog's good health is to maintain a sensible routine. Good nutrition, adequate exercise, and regular checkups are essential to a senior dog's health. Although aging is inevitable, there are a few things you can to do slow the process down a bit. These include having your dog's teeth professionally cleaned (periodontal disease can lead to a number of serious illnesses), teaching him new tricks every now and then to keep his mind sharp (yes, old dogs can learn new ones!), and increasing the frequency of his routine veterinary checkups to twice yearly.

The Cockapoo's pendulous ears can leave him vulnerable to ear infections.

an increased risk when both parent breeds harbor a tendency to develop a particular condition. Rest assured that a crossbred dog possesses no higher chance of developing a common illness to both his parent breeds than a dog of either purebred. Still, you will need to watch out for your dog's predisposed afflictions just as the owner of a purebred dog would. These are a few of the problems your designer dog might face.

Allergies

Of the designer dogs covered in this book, the ones most prone to allergies are the Cavachon and Cockapoo, but any dog may suffer from this uncomfortable situation.

Just like people, many dogs suffer from food allergies. Also similar to the problem in humans, identifying canine allergens can be rather time consuming. Although allergy tests are available, often the most effective route is good old-fashioned trial and error. If your dog's tummy seems to be consistently upset by his food, begin removing as few ingredients at once as possible (ideally just one at a time) and watching for any physical reactions. If no improvement is noticed after several days, return that item to your dog's diet and remove another until you can isolate the problem-causing agent. Common canine food allergens are corn and wheat, but because every dog is different, the problem could

literally be anything. The best way to avoid this painstaking identification process is to introduce new foods to your dog slowly, one at a time.

Other common canine allergies involve skin reactions. Sometimes smaller dogs are prone to skin problems related to allergies, but regular grooming (especially brushing) can help to prevent these issues. Bear in mind, however, that bathing too frequently (or without a shampoo created to help a particular problem) can often aggravate a skin irritation. If your dog experiences severe itching, redness, or a rash, schedule an appointment with your veterinarian to determine the cause.

Ear Infections

Like his parent breeds, the Cocker Spaniel and Poodle, the Cockapoo has pendulous ears, leaving him particularly vulnerable to ear infections. With the ear leather lying so closely against the ear canal, airflow is severely restricted; this results in trapped moisture, a breeding ground for infection. Though usually caused by bacteria or yeast, ear infections known as otitis externa also can result from wax buildup, an overabundance of hair inside the ear, or a foreign body that has become lodged in the ear canal. They also can be secondary to other kinds of bodily infections. When otitis externa spreads to the middle ear, the result is otitis media, a more serious infection. A ruptured eardrum also can cause otitis media.

The signs of an ear infection are nearly unmistakable. Your dog will likely shake his head or scratch at his head uncontrollably in response to the discomfort. Tilting of the head in one direction is also a sign of an ear infection. The ear itself may appear red or swollen, with or without a black or yellowish discharge. Often there is also a strong, offensive odor emanating from the ear.

At the first sign of an ear infection, bring your dog to his veterinarian for an examination. As tempting as it may be to clean the ear before heading to the vet, refrain from doing so. Even a mild cleanser will irritate your dog's already sore ear. Your vet also may need to swab the area to confirm the diagnosis. An antibiotic will then be prescribed. Ear infections do not subside without proper treatment, so always seek veterinary care. Although rare, a serious infection left untreated can result in loss of hearing.

Epilepsy

Designer dogs who are prone to idiopathic epilepsy (meaning there is no known reason for the seizures) include the Cavachon, Cockapoo, Goldendoodle, Labradoodle, and Schnoodle.

Witnessing a canine seizure can be extremely scary for an unsuspecting owner, but there is usually no way to predict if or when your dog will experience this kind of incident.

A seizing animal may shake, appear dizzy, or even fall down. In some instances, there is a loss of bladder or bowel control as well. As difficult as it may sound, the best thing you can do for your dog in this situation is to remain calm. In fact, by paying close attention to the circumstances surrounding the seizure, you may be able to avert a future attack.

Not all dogs who experience a seizure are necessarily suffering from epilepsy. Seizing also can be a symptom of several other conditions, including allergies, low blood sugar (hypoglycemia), or occasionally even more serious problems, such as tumors. It is very important that you report a

The Best Health Care Tip: Be Proactive!

Bringing your dog for veterinary visits and checking him over yourself for red-flag symptoms are both important steps in proper pet care, but even better is preventing illness in the first place. As a society, we have become so obsessed with problem solving that we often forget the best approach to any problem is prevention. Want to prevent your pup from suffering from ear infections? Be sure to clean his ears at least once a week. Worried that your overly zealous eater may become obese, a condition that can lead to countless other health problems? Select a quality weight-maintenance food for him. Also, pick up a measuring cup to keep in the kibble container so that you are sure to offer modest and consistent servings—after going for a brisk walk, of course. To prevent your dog from falling ill due to toxins in his environment, reduce the number of chemicals you use in and around your home. Clean with vinegar or other natural products. Always wipe your feet before entering your home—or better yet, remove your shoes; this can seriously limit the amount of pesticides brought into your family's home. You may not use chemicals to treat your own lawn, but consider how many places you walk each day that do. Continue adding new proactive steps like these to your household routine, and you will help to keep canine health problems from striking.

seizure to your dog's veterinarian for this reason.

If the problem is indeed epilepsy, there are several approaches a vet may take. In many cases, medical treatment is not even necessary. If the seizures occur too frequently, for long periods of time (a seizure lasting more than a minute or two is considered significant), or if the episodes are extremely intense, an anticonvulsant medication may be prescribed. When not a secondary problem, most canine seizures will not prevent a dog from living an otherwise normal life.

Eye Problems

Cataracts

A great many designer dogs are susceptible to cataracts. These include the Cavachon, Cockapoo, Goldendoodle, Pekeapoo, Schnoodle, and Yorkipoo. Fortunately, cataracts are painless and highly treatable. A cataract is an opaque spot on the lens or capsule of the eye that usually causes impairment of vision or blindness. Cataracts that are dense enough to interfere with the dog's vision are usually extremely noticeable to an observant owner. This

condition may be inherited or caused by a traumatic injury to the dog's eye. The latter situation will only affect the eye that has been wounded. Although there is no way to prevent or reverse cataracts, they can be surgically removed and replaced with an acrylic lens by a veterinary ophthalmologist. This procedure offers an impressive success rate of 90 to 95 percent in otherwise healthy dogs. Interestingly, this statistic remains the same regardless of how long a dog has had cataracts.

Glaucoma

You may often hear glaucoma mentioned together with cataracts, but these are in fact two different diseases. Unlike cataracts, which technically don't require treatment, glaucoma is a serious disease that demands immediate medical attention. Also unlike cataracts, glaucoma can be painful. Although any designer dog or purebred can suffer from glaucoma, Cockapoos are especially prone to this problem.

Caused by intraocular pressure (pressure within the dog's eyeball), glaucoma may present with redness, cloudiness, tearing, loss of vision, an enlarged eyeball, uncharacteristic aggressiveness, lethargy, or loss of appetite. The

Some Schnoodles are prone to cataracts.

This Pekeapoo puppy has tons of energy; just make sure that your puppy is not overexercising.

disease is most often congenital, but in rare cases it can be caused by a coexisting condition: a luxating (floating) lens that blocks the natural fluid drainage of the dog's eye. Regardless of its cause, glaucoma can result in irreversible vision loss within mere hours if the pressure is not relieved.

Progressive Retinal Degeneration (PRD)

Unfortunately, not all diseases that cause blindness can be alleviated with early intervention or surgical procedures. Progressive retinal degeneration (PRD) is an inherited disorder that causes gradual but inevitable vision loss. This is caused by the deterioration of the retina. Designer dogs commonly affected by PRD include Schnoodles and Labradoodles.

A dog with PRD will begin bumping into things at night or in low-light situations, but he will eventually show signs of increasing vision loss, regardless of the time of day or light quality. Other symptoms are usually barely noticeable until the disease has already reached an advanced stage.

Although it is natural for an owner to feel overwhelmed at first by the prognosis of permanent blindness, it is important to realize that your dog will be impacted by this deficit far less than a human being in a similar situation. Blind dogs can live enormously satisfying lives. Although some additional training may be necessary, most sightless dogs acclimate to this change easily by simply doing what they have always done: relying on their other, more valued senses—chiefly hearing and smell.

Sterilization: The Mother of All Cancer Prevention

I often look at my dog Molly and think what a wonderful mother she would have made. Whenever there is a puppy in our home, she instantly assumes the role of a doting parent. When our family watched Molly's eight-week-old half-brother, Finnegan, for a few days while his owner had to work, Molly helped with everything from housetraining to bodyguard duty.

At these heartwarming moments, it could be easy to wonder if my husband and I made the right decision when we had Molly spayed. We are confident, though, that having Molly fixed was the best gift we could have ever given her. Statistically, spayed and neutered dogs live longer lives. In females sterilization eliminates the possibility of uterine and ovarian cancer, and it greatly reduces the risk of a number of other health problems—including breast cancer. Similarly, neutering male dogs effectively prevents testicular cancer and significantly lessens their chance of suffering from prostate cancer. Additionally, sterilized dogs typically make better pets. They are more affectionate and less likely to exhibit problem behaviors. Because the world is already filled with countless dogs in need of homes, we are content to allow Molly to look after our friends' puppies to fulfill any maternal instincts she may have—and at the end of the day, she seems pretty satisfied to see them go home and have her family back to herself.

Hip Dysplasia

Hip dysplasia is a common problem in Cockapoos, Goldendoodles, and Labradoodles. This condition occurs when the hip joint is not properly formed. This may result from a genetic predisposition or from environmental factors. Because the average age of onset is two years (the problem is nearly impossible to diagnose in dogs younger than six months old), it is extremely important that owners ask potential breeders for documentation that a puppy's parents and grandparents have been screened for hip dysplasia. Only dogs who have received official clearance from the Orthopedic Foundation

for Animals (OFA) should be bred. Because the condition is not always genetic, however, even the most careful selection of parents cannot guarantee that your pup will not develop hip dysplasia.

The best way to prevent hip dysplasia is by providing your dog with a sensible fitness plan. Overweight dogs are particularly prone to dysplasia, so overfeeding can increase your dog's risk. While exercise should be part of virtually any dog's routine, *over-exercising* also can expose your dog to this problem (especially in younger dogs), so make sure that your dog isn't overdoing it either. Injuries also can increase the incidence of hip dysplasia.

The most common symptom of hip dysplasia is pain or discomfort, especially first thing in the morning or directly following exercise. If you notice your dog limping or avoiding activity, it may be time to have him checked. By seeking treatment early, you will likely be able to relieve your pet's pain, return him to greater mobility, and prevent the unnecessary loss of muscle tone.

Once an X-ray confirms the diagnosis, a treatment plan must be chosen. In more serious cases, surgery may be necessary. Sometimes, though, owners can improve their dogs' prognosis by making small changes. If your dog is too heavy, reducing his weight is a great place to start. Additionally, exercise that focuses on range of motion and muscle building can be extremely helpful, providing it limits stress on your dog's joints. Providing your dog with warm, comfortable sleeping quarters, utilizing massage and physical therapy, and taking simple steps to make his everyday activities less painful also can be beneficial.

Patellar Luxation

As your dog's leg bends and straightens normally, his patella (the technical term for the kneecap) slides up and down within a groove in his femur. When the kneecap slips out of this groove, it is called patellar luxation. Pomchis are especially vulnerable to this condition. The causes for this problem can vary and may include such possibilities as a malformation of the groove itself.

Luxation, or dislocation, may happen over and over or it might only happen occasionally, so treatment will depend on the intensity of the problem. If the problem is only intermittent, it may require only a simple adjustment by your veterinarian. If luxation is chronically repetitive, however, surgery may be necessary. Osteoarthritis also can develop over time if the condition persists.

More common in smaller dogs, patellar luxation is relatively easy to spot and usually manifests itself by the time a dog is six months old. A dog with this problem will appear lame for no apparent reason—or merely hop for a few steps at a time if the problem is a sporadic one.

Although surgical prognosis can vary, most dogs return to full

Breeding puppies (like this Puggle) is best left to experts.

do notice any abnormalities, notify your dog's veterinarian immediately. It is important to note, however, that not all cancers present themselves in obvious ways, so keep an eye on your dog's overall health and behavior in addition to being on the lookout for unusual growths.

One of the best ways to prevent your dog from being diagnosed with cancer is spaying or neutering your dog early. Spaying your female puppy will prevent her from being stricken with ovarian cancer, and it may significantly lessen her risk for mammary tumors, as well. Neutering your male dog will similarly prevent testicular cancer.

72

function provided that activity is properly limited during the recovery period.

General Illnesses

Cancer

No one likes to hear the word *cancer*. Being told that your dog has a malignancy can be devastating. What it doesn't have to be, however, is a death sentence. Mast cell tumors, one of the most common forms of canine cancer, can frequently be removed with an excellent prognosis.

Early detection of cancer, perhaps more so than any other affliction, is crucial. By checking your dog frequently for any suspicious lumps or bumps, you increase his chances of beating this brutal disease. If you

Hypothyroidism

A sudden weight gain can often signal a medical problem. If your dog's food intake or lack of exercise is clearly the cause, a diet and exercise plan may be all that's needed to reverse the situation. If, however, you notice an increase in weight for no apparent reason, ask your veterinarian if hypothyroidism could be the explanation.

In addition to weight gain, dry skin and hair loss are also signs of this endocrine disorder. When the thyroid gland is underactive, your dog's metabolism decreases, making it easier for him to gain weight. The typical age of onset is between four and ten years. Once a diagnosis has been made, treatment with a synthetic thyroid hormone is usually used. Although periodic blood samples should be taken to ensure proper treatment, this condition is usually highly manageable.

Parasites

Fleas

Though not usually thought of as a dangerous problem, flea bites can lead to a number of serious canine health problems, including parasitic infections. By protecting your dog with a monthly flea and tick preventive, you can easily avoid a painful and exasperating infestation and possibly several other health issues.

Heartworm

A serious problem that can be avoided easily with proper preventive treatment is heartworm. Transmitted through mosquito bites, heartworm disease progresses rapidly. By the time an owner notices symptoms, it has usually progressed to a precarious stage. Monthly prevention is highly preferable. Because mosquitoes have been known to breed in temperatures as low as 57°F (14°C), year-round treatment is recommended in many parts of the country.

Ticks

Lyme disease has quickly become the most notorious tick-related illness in the US. Whenever outdoors, I am constantly checking my dogs for the frighteningly small deer ticks that transmit this incurable illness. While owners should certainly remain vigilant of the dreaded deer tick, we mustn't overlook the other equally menacing tick varieties that can cause your dog (and your human family members) to become ill. Among the other diseases that ticks can transmit are Rocky Mountain spotted fever, encephalitis, tularemia, and tick paralysis. Although ticks are sluggish and incapable of flight, even larger ones can be easily overlooked even on a short-haired dog. This is why you should always examine your dog thoroughly whenever coming in from the great outdoors.

If you find a tick on your dog, use a pair of tweezers to carefully remove it. Because it is vital that you get both the tick's head and body out, your first objective will be getting the tick to simply let go on its own. To do this, use a pair of sterilized tweezers to

Check your dog for fleas and ticks after he's been outside—this Cavachon is happy to be bug free!

Be Prepared

Like a Boy Scout, you should always be prepared. This means having a disaster kit in your home as well as a smaller version in the trunk of your car if your pet routinely rides with you. The kit should include a week's supply of food and water in nonbreakable, airtight containers to ensure safety and freshness. You should replace this food and water every six months and rethink your pet's needs for the kit once a year to make sure that the supplies meet your current needs—the same collar that fits your new puppy is not likely to fit him a year later.

If you pack canned food, make sure that you have a handheld can opener, too. And don't forget a plastic dish that can double as a food and water dish. An extra collar and leash are also important things to have in your kit. You also should have a portable kennel for each of your pets handy. The San Francisco Society for the Prevention of Cruelty to Animals says that the official Red Cross policy is that there are no animals allowed in emergency shelters, but they have been known to make exceptions if the animal is securely confined. You will want to make certain that you have a well-stocked first-aid kit for your pet that includes tweezers, gauze bandages, first-aid cream, antiseptic spray, and hydrogen peroxide. Ask your veterinarian about storing any medications that your pet may need to take regularly.

Courtesy of the American Animal Hospital Association and Healthypet.com

Designer Dogs

grasp the tick's body and begin pulling it away from your dog's skin very gently. Apply steady pressure, but be sure not to squeeze too tightly. Jiggling the tick a bit is fine, but don't rotate it.

Pulling too hard or twisting can cause the tick's body to separate from its head, which can remain embedded in your pet and leave him vulnerable to infection. If this happens, contact your veterinarian for further instruction. Some vets suggest using a drop or two of isopropyl alcohol to get a tick to release a stubborn grip, but according to the American Lyme Disease Foundation (ALDF), this method can backfire, even increasing the chances

of disease transmission. Once the tick is out, this is the time for the alcohol— drop the tick in some of this solution to kill it. Never use your bare hands or feet to kill a tick. As soon as the tick has been properly disposed of, clean the bite wound with disinfectant and sterilize your tweezers with some fresh alcohol.

Complementary Therapies

Once categorized as alternative medicine, techniques such as acupuncture and chiropractic care are becoming more and more popular. One of the biggest advantages to these complementary treatments, also called holistic medicine, is that they aim to treat the whole animal. (The word *holistic* actually means *whole*.) Most holistic caregivers believe that there is a deep connection between the body and the mind and that finding balance between the two is essential for true healing. Many pet owners are seeing for themselves how these ancient modalities can be used effectively in conjunction with more conventional modern veterinary care.

CST

Craniosacral therapy (CST) is a modality that focuses on natural healing by seeking to restore balance to the membranes and fluid surrounding the brain and spinal cord, also called the craniosacral region. Performed by gently placing their hands on the dog's neck and head, CST caregivers follow a specific path and observe the body's subtle responses, or the animal's craniosacral rhythm. Through this movement, the body is stimulated to correct the problem. CST is used primarily to treat balance problems and neurological disorders.

Homeopathy

An increasing number of veterinarians offer complementary services, but it is important that anyone practicing these techniques be properly trained, so always ask about a particular person's credentials before allowing her to treat your pet. Homeopathy, for

Complementary therapies can often help dogs like this Labradoodle.

instance, is the method of treating an illness with a minute amount of the very substance that in greater amounts would normally cause the affliction in a healthy individual. The objective of this therapy is to stimulate the body's natural healing response, similar to the way a vaccination works. The dosing, however, is crucial. The potency of any homeopathic treatment is even greater when smaller amounts are used. This makes extensive knowledge and experience an absolute necessity. You don't have to be a veterinarian to perform homeopathy, and just because someone has the letters DVM after their name doesn't mean that she is qualified.

Massage and Hydrotherapy

You may not even realize that physical therapy is a complementary procedure because it has become such a mainstream approach, but the roots of this common treatment also lie in ancient times. Massage and hydrotherapy (techniques involving water) have been around for thousands of years. They too should be done only by a properly trained caregiver. Because there is currently no licensing requirement for canine physical therapists—and the human and canine bodies are so different—the most ideal caregivers are veterinarians who also have been certified in human physical therapy.

Tui Na

Another form of holistic treatment that is growing in popularity is Tui Na, a cross between Chinese acupressure and massage. This technique can help

to alleviate joint, musculoskeletal, and nerve pain. Like many holistic treatments, it is also used to strengthen the immune system, the most basic weapon in fighting countless ailments.

At one time complementary medicine was tainted with the connotation of being eccentric or desperate. Fortunately, this is changing. Used for wellness care as well as treating disease and injury, these age-old techniques are proving their effectiveness with their staying power. Your pet also may need conventional veterinary care alongside these modalities, but this is the very essence of the complementary approach: being open to the particular combination of remedies that work best for your individual dog's needs. To find a holistic veterinarian in your area, contact the American Holistic Veterinary Medical Association (AHVMA) at www.holisticvetlist.com.

In Case of Emergency

sembling a fully stocked first-aid kit is a smart safety precaution. The following
ould always be kept on hand, but remember that nothing replaces the expertise
terinarian. Although you may be tempted to frantically browse your canine first-
anual or go online in search of quick advice that might help your dog if he is sic
jured, the time-sensitive nature of an emergency demands that your dog receive
re of a trained professional as soon as possible. In the event of a medical crisis,
ur veterinary hospital at once. Your first-aid kit will likely come in handy once y
ve received instructions from the staff, but there is no substitute for the knowle
d experience of a trained professional.

- antibiotic ointment
- canine first-aid manual
- children's diphenhydramine (antihistamine)
- cotton swabs
- emergency phone numbers (including poison control, emergency veterinarian, and your dog's regular vet)
- flashlight
- hydrogen peroxide
- instant ice pack
- pecac syrup

- nonstick gauze pads, gauze, and tap
- oral syringe or eyedropper (plastic, glass)
- rectal thermometer
- saline solution
- scissors
- soap
- styptic powder or pencil
- tweezers
- any other item your veterinarian recommends keeping on hand

member to keep an eye on expiration dates, and toss any products before they s

Chapter 6

Being Good

Nearly all well-mannered dogs have one thing in common: Their owners have made training a priority. Good behavior is no accident. Whether you are in the midst of housetraining a new puppy or finally teaching your two-year-old Goldendoodle how to walk on his leash, you cannot achieve your goal unless you can properly convey it to your pet in a way he understands. On its most basic level, this is what training is—effective communication between you and your pet.

Socialization

Dogs are social creatures. Like people, though, they must be exposed to other dogs and humans regularly to remain comfortable and trustworthy in a variety of social situations. The best way to accomplish this is by including your dog in as many of your own activities as possible. From bringing your pet along as you walk your child to school to allowing your dog to welcome company to your home, making your dog a part of your daily experiences will enrich his people skills and provide him with the positive interaction he needs.

While your dog is still a puppy, encourage well-behaved children to pet him, and consider planning pet-friendly activities with friends who are also dog owners. The earlier he is exposed to other people and animals, the better.

If you are a homebody, start getting out for regular walks with your dog every day. You will be surprised by the people and animals you encounter just in your own neighborhood. Say hello to them, and ask if they would be willing to offer your dog a treat. Bringing treats along for strangers to give your dog is a great way to help him associate people with pleasure. If a person is fearful of dogs or if your dog appears to take an instant dislike to a particular individual, though, bid that person a quick farewell and keep walking. Your goal is a positive and safe experience for all involved.

Crate Training

Crate training has many advantages for

Socializing your dog is very important—these Pekeapoos know how to interact with different types of dogs and people.

both dogs and their owners. It is an excellent means of jumpstarting the housetraining process and a smart way to protect your furniture and other belongings from being destroyed when you aren't able to properly supervise your new pet. It also provides your dog with a quiet retreat of his own, something dogs seek out. Think of how often you find your dog snoozing under the dining room table or in a dark corner of the room.

Getting Started

Begin by simply placing the crate in your home. Ideally, the crate should be there even before you bring your puppy home. Leave the door open so that your dog can investigate the enclosure. You can pique his interest by leaving a special toy or other treat inside the enclosure. Don't shut the door as soon as he enters, though.

Once he seems comfortable being inside the kennel, you may start closing the door for short periods, just a few minutes at a time in the beginning. This duration should gradually increase as you continue crate training your dog. If he cries when you close the door, resist the urge to open it too quickly, as this will only teach him that fussing will get him what he wants. Instead, wait for when he stops, even if the silence lasts only a moment. It is imperative that you end on a positive

The Expert Knows

Does My Dog Have to Go Outside?

Yes! If you live in a cold climate, you may find it practical to train your Pomchi to use a litter box, but getting outside for fresh air on warmer days is important for all dogs. Also, just because your dog is diminutive in stature doesn't mean that he prefers to be carried all the time. Allowing your dog to don a leash and explore your neighborhood is one of the best gifts you can give him. While a small dog's exercise needs are certainly less considerable than a larger one's, a Pekeapoo still needs to run and play to be healthy, just like a Goldendoodle does. You may even find that going for a daily walk with your dog can help to improve his mood and behavior.

note—and always praise him for showing patience.

I never put my own dogs in their crates without first grabbing a small treat for them. They have gotten so accustomed to this, in fact, that as soon as a cookie hits my hand, they immediately head to their crates. I find that this is a fun way to say goodbye, so my dogs *almost* look forward to my leaving the house each day.

How Long?

As your dog acclimates to his crate, you will start noticing him using it more and more. This is a wonderful sign that the crate training period is nearing its end. No dog should ever be left in his crate

Don't Spring Your Dog From His Crate!

Avoid rushing to open the door to your dog's crate the moment you return home—or making a big fuss over the event—or he may look forward to being let out of his kennel a bit too much. Show your dog that you are happy to see him, of course, but wait just a minute or two for him to calm down first.

with the door closed for more than a few hours at a time, though, no matter how well he tolerates it. In addition to needing regular potty breaks, your dog needs time to stretch his legs and play. If you must be away from home for an excessive amount of time, be sure to have a friend or family member stop by to provide these important opportunities.

Housetraining

If you are using a crate, you are already halfway to successful housetraining. Because dogs instinctually prefer not to soil the area in which they sleep, placing your dog in his crate will discourage accidents when you cannot watch him. You must, however, provide regular opportunities for him to eliminate in the appropriate place. When your puppy is just eight weeks old, this will mean taking him outside every two hours for a chance to relieve himself. You may extend this time by an hour for every four additional weeks of age. Of course, there is a limit to

this increase. No dog should ever have to wait more than six to eight hours between elimination trips. You also should give your dog an opportunity to relieve himself both before entering his crate and again once he exits.

When you take your dog to his potty spot, give him a few minutes to do his business. The moment he begins eliminating, say the word or phrase you would like him to link with the activity and praise him excitedly. Be careful not to use this word too soon, however, or your dog may have a harder time learning what it means. Eventually, you may be able to teach him to eliminate on command by using this word.

If your dog hasn't eliminated after several minutes, take him back indoors. Watch him carefully as you wait about 20 minutes before attaching his leash and heading back outside together. As taxing as this initial routine can be, bear in mind that he *will* go eventually. By keeping an eye on both your dog and the clock, you can help to ensure that he eliminates where he should.

Choosing not to crate train does not mean that housetraining will be more difficult for your dog; it will simply require a bit more vigilance on your behalf. Before I began using crates, I found baby gates extremely useful for this purpose. In the beginning I still had to watch my puppy closely, but once she could be trusted for short periods of time, a gate made it possible to at least contain the threat of accidents to my linoleum when another responsibility beckoned.

Dealing With Accidents

Whether you choose to crate your dog or not, you will inevitably have to clean up after him from time to time until he is reliably housetrained. For this essential task, a product made specifically to absorb pet odors will be helpful, but this will only be effective once you have fully soaked up all the wetness. Even more important than thoroughly cleaning up the mess, though, is abstaining from punishing your pet. Instead, praise him when he eliminates in the proper spot.

Once you discover an accident, remove your pet from the room immediately. Again, this is an instance when a crate comes in handy. If you don't use one, simply place your dog in another room and close the door before you grab the paper towels. If allowed to watch the clean-up process, your dog may get the impression that

his job is to make the mess and yours is to clean it up.

Housetraining takes time and patience. It certainly isn't the most enjoyable part of dog ownership, but it doesn't have to be a grueling process for either you or your dog. By establishing a schedule and sticking to it, you will make it easier on both of you. And by praising your dog whenever he eliminates in the correct spot, you will show him that success feels good.

Basic Commands

One of the best ways to get your dog to repeat virtually any behavior is by offering him a reward when he performs a particular task. (Keep this in

Supervision is essential for successful housetraining. This Pekeapoo is never out of sight!

mind if you ever consider offering your dog a treat to stop him from barking!) Timing is crucial. Offering a reward either too soon or too late can reinforce the wrong behavior, and feeding overly large or chewy treats also can impede your progress. The treats used as rewards for training must be small and easy for your dog to consume quickly. If they aren't, you lose valuable training time and risk distracting your pet from the task at hand.

Training for excessively long periods of time also can hinder your dog's success. Work with your pet at different times throughout each day instead of devoting an entire block of time to training. Begin with 5-minute sessions, and increase this period to a maximum of 15 minutes if your dog is remaining engaged in the activity. If you feel that he can tolerate more training time,

increase the number of sessions, not the duration.

Sit

Sit is one of the easiest commands to teach a dog, as evidenced by the plethora of pups whose rumps hit the floor the instant they hear the rattle of their cookie jar covers. If your dog has yet to learn this most basic training task, grab that dog cookie and hold it up in the air as you gently move it back over your dog's head. Most dogs will naturally move into the sitting position at this time. When yours does, say the word *sit*. Offer praise along with the tasty treat as soon as he sits. Of course, you will need to repeat this exercise many times, but this simple position is the basis for teaching numerous other training tasks.

Stay

Once your dog consistently sits on command, you can begin teaching him to stay. After issuing the *sit* command, raise your hand and say the word *stay* as you back up very slowly. In the beginning your dog may only remain still for a few seconds, but it is especially important to offer praise during this time, however short. One of the biggest mistakes owners make when teaching their dogs the *stay* command is making it easy for the dogs to do just the opposite. If your pet begins to move, immediately get in his way. Once he relaxes again, though, you should begin stepping back again.

Gradually increase the number of steps you take away from your dog. You also should increase the amount of time before you offer praise or a reward. Eventually, your dog should be able to stay for about a minute or longer with you at least 10 feet (3 m) away.

Down

Down is another command for which teaching your dog to sit is a prerequisite. Edible rewards are also helpful props for this training task. With your dog in the sitting position, hold onto his collar with one of your hands as you hold a treat in front of your dog with the other. Slowly begin lowering the treat, waiting to say the word *down* until the moment your dog's chest hits the floor. You may then give him the treat and praise him lavishly. Once you have performed the task this way several times, try removing the treat. Continue dispensing praise, though, for

nothing is a greater incentive for a dog than pleasing his owner.

Come

The easiest way to teach your dog to come to you is by capitalizing on this common occurrence whenever it happens naturally. As soon as you

FAMILY-FRIENDLY TIP

In-Home Help

Children love to share in the fun of training the family dog. Remembering the appropriate times to provide praise or a treat, however, can be a challenge for kids. To ensure that your dog learns his commands as he should, delegate. The first person to teach your dog a new command should be a knowledgeable adult or adolescent. Once you notice that your dog has begun to catch on, you may then defer practice sessions to a younger family member. If your child is particularly young, place her in charge of calling your dog for his training session or playing a rewarding game of fetch with him afterward. This makes it possible for everyone to participate in training without confusing your pet by reinforcing the wrong behaviors.

This Cavachon can go many fun places because he knows how to walk nicely on a leash.

notice your dog moving your way, tell him "Come!" in a cheerful voice and reward him for following through with his own plan. The more your dog hears the command in conjunction with the behavior, the quicker he will learn it. You also can practice by using the *come* command from across a large room or backyard, but you must have a means of making your dog comply if

Finding a Trainer

Two of your best resources for finding a first-rate dog trainer are your veterinarian and your local humane society. You also can contact the Association of Pet Dog Trainers (APDT) at (800) PET-DOGS or www.apdt.com for the name of a trainer in your area.

he does not obey. In this case, another person can lead him to you, or you can use an extendable leash. The latter tool will be necessary if you are working outdoors without the safety of a fence.

Always be aware of your body language while teaching your dog any command, but especially *come*. Even when your mood is low, show your dog that you are happy to see him when he comes to you. Most importantly, no matter what he has done, never admonish him when he comes—or he may not come to you when noncompliance could be dangerous. Oftentimes it helps to get down to your dog's level when calling him. This welcoming posture mimics the canine play bow, the stance dogs use to initiate play.

Heel

You may think that teaching a dog to heel is only useful if you intend to participate in obedience trials with him, but owners who have no such plans can certainly enjoy the benefits of teaching their pets this command, too. Although it sounds rather technical, the *heel* command is really just a means of training a dog how to walk on a leash. It can be frustrating to walk a dog—even a small one—who insists on pulling the entire way. In addition to being tiresome for you, pulling can be dangerous to your pet, especially if he is a tiny designer dog with a delicate neck, such as a Pomchi or a Pekeapoo.

If your dog can sit, he can heel. Begin by attaching his leash and walking him on your left side with the leash in your right hand and a treat in your left. When you stop, say the word *sit*. When he complies, reward him and say the word *heel.* Then begin walking again, stopping periodically to practice this two-part exercise. Your ultimate goal is for your dog to comfortably walk alongside you, stopping whenever you do.

Practice Makes Perfect

Once your dog has mastered these basic commands, you can help to reinforce them by practicing in different places. Getting your dog to sit and stay in your living room is much easier than eliciting the same result in a noisy or otherwise distracting environment. Learning new commands also can be great fun for your pet. It gives him a chance to show you how smart he is, so continue to make training part of his regular routine even after he masters the basics.

SENIOR DOG TIP

Adult Learners

The techniques for training an older dog need not differ from the approach you'd use for a younger pet. For a dog with a few more years behind him, however, patience is especially important, as is persistence. Perhaps you have adopted an adult dog who was never properly trained by his previous owner. You may find that he enjoys the extra time and attention that training provides, but this doesn't mean that success will come quickly. Maybe the reason his previous training didn't stick was because the owner didn't stick with it. Show your new pet that you are in it for the long haul. Praise even his small accomplishments, and continue working on one task at a time until he has mastered each one. Sessions also do not need to be long. Spending just a few minutes each day—every day—is highly preferable to trying to jam a week's worth of training into a Saturday afternoon.

87

Being Good

Chapter 7

In the
Doghouse

Preventing problem behaviors is one of the most important things you will ever do as a pet owner. When your dog acts appropriately, both you and he can enjoy your time together instead of feeling frustrated or ashamed by his actions. A well-behaved pet is also welcome in more places than a less reliable one, expanding the list of activities the two of you can share. Reversing problems like excessive barking and inappropriate chewing can be intimidating tasks, but ignoring issues like these will inevitably only make them worse.

Chewing

The most important thing to remember about chewing is that it is actually a healthy canine pastime. As long as your dog is chewing appropriate items belonging to him, there is no reason to redirect him. In fact, younger dogs should even be encouraged to chew bones and other hard toys to ease the pain of teething and to relieve stress and boredom right through adulthood. If your dog is making toast of your tennis shoes, though, there is no time to waste.

Solution

Each time you see your dog grab hold of an item that is not his, gently remove it from his mouth before replacing the object with an appropriate belonging of his own. When he accepts this substitute, praise him. If the item doesn't seem to hold his attention, keep looking for toys that do engage him. Whatever you do, never allow one of your possessions to become a hand-me-down chew toy. While your decimated sneakers may be of no further use to you, passing them to your dog will be counterproductive in teaching him what is and isn't appropriate for chewing.

When you can't watch your dog, you must have a way of keeping him from munching on your property. Crates work best for this, but baby gates also can be helpful. Just making sure that tempting objects are kept out of your dog's reach can help to prevent him from chewing inappropriately. And once you replace this bad habit with

Have any sudden change in behavior checked out by your vet. (This Chiweenie is feeling fine—it's just his "serious" face!)

the healthier practice of utilizing chew toys, you may eventually be able to be a bit less meticulous about placing all your things out of your dog's reach.

Digging

Some designer dogs are more prone to digging than others. Labradoodles, for example, are natural diggers. Akin with their innate talent for search and rescue, these dogs can smell a mouse or a frog—or virtually anything—from several feet (m) above the ground, and they make no bones about going after whatever it is. While this ability can be heroic when applied in the proper way, you may feel far less appreciative of it when you see the unearthed roots of your lilac bush or a pile of dirt beside what was once the home of your lady slippers.

Solution

Digging can be one of the most difficult problem behaviors to correct, but it can be done. Like barking, there is nothing inherently wrong about digging, so some owners don't feel a need to eliminate the behavior entirely, but rather limit it to an appropriate area. By providing their dogs with a small spot where they can dig, these owners indulge one of their dogs' most basic instincts while protecting their own gardens in the process. If your dog moves from this area, merely redirect him to his own spot.

Another useful approach is the art of distraction. Although a dog may

To keep your Pekeapoo— and tulips—safe, designate an area specifically for your dog to dig in.

enjoy digging, providing him with other means of amusing himself can help to show him that other activities also can be fun. Use balls, squeak toys, and nylon bones to divert your dog's attention if digging becomes an obsession, and be sure to play with him as much as you can. Many unpleasant behaviors result from

Finding a Behaviorist

Although a certification process for animal behaviorists does exist, there are currently only a limited number of certified individuals. You can find a directory at www. animalbehavior.org. You also can ask your veterinarian, trainer, or local humane society to recommend a behaviorist.

Don't Wait!

When it comes to correcting any canine problem behavior, your dog's perspective is just as important as your own. It is essential that he sees you as his alpha pack member, his superior. If you have adopted an older dog, you must make it your first priority to establish your position with your new pet—just as you would for a puppy. You do this by providing him with both structure and love. Any adopted pet may need an adjustment period, but you mustn't confuse this acclimation process with an excuse to postpone training. Being patient and kind should certainly be part of your approach, but the best way to help your dog adjust to his new home is by providing him with a consistent routine. If he needs remedial housetraining, begin working on this immediately. If he growls at you when you go near his food dish, start hand feeding him tonight. By allowing him a few weeks to settle in before you address an issue, you will only be allowing the problem to intensify into an even more serious one.

boredom, but digging is a bit different. Boredom can certainly exacerbate this behavior, but it doesn't cause it. So a combination of these two approaches is usually best.

Excessive Barking

Barking itself is not a bad thing. Using barking to alert his owner to the presence of strangers or to ask to be walked are ways a dog *should* be using his voice. A pet who barks excessively, though, can elicit complaints from neighbors, trouble with landlords, and even visits from the police. Listening to a dog—even your own—bark incessantly is not fun. Teaching him when barking is and isn't acceptable is the goal here.

Solution

Before you can help your dog understand that you want him to stop barking, you first need to teach him to bark on command. This may seem foolish since he has obviously already mastered the art of barking, but if you can't get him to bark during training, it will be impossible to reward the desired behavior: stopping.

With two treats in hand, knock on a door or other surface within your home as you say "Speak!" As soon your dog complies, offer him one reward. The moment he stops, say "Enough" as you give him the second treat. It is crucial that you wait until the instant he stops barking. Providing the reward just a moment too soon—or even slightly too late—can make your dog relate the treat to the wrong action.

Once your dog knows the *enough*

command, you can use it whenever he barks for too long in your presence. To

Barking is your dog's way of communicating— the enough command helps curb this Labradoodle's barking.

some degree your dog will replace his barking habit with this more abbreviated means of expressing himself. For the times when you are not available to stop him, though, you will need a back-up plan. This can be tailored to suit your individual dog. If he tends to bark when he sees people walking by your home, restrict his access to the windows. If noise is the trigger, leave a radio or television on to offset the sound. Also, be sure to always leave him with interactive toys (and rotate them regularly!) to help him pass the time when you can't be with him. Many dogs bark or howl out of boredom when left alone.

House Soiling

House soiling, or housetraining regression, is one of the most exasperating of all problem behaviors. Especially if your dog had previously succeeded at eliminating in the proper spot, finding unwanted puddles or droppings inside your home can leave you feeling confused as to what has caused this unpleasant step backward. This can actually lead you to a solution, however. Taking a closer look at the reason your dog might be urinating or defecating where he shouldn't is the first step in solving the problem, and your first phone call should be to your vet. Many serious health

problems present with symptoms of incontinence. Once you can rule out a physical cause for the problem, you can then begin adjusting your dog's routine for remedial training.

Solution

A healthy adult dog should be able to go several hours between trips for elimination. When your goal is stopping house soiling, however, you must begin taking your dog to his potty spot more often than he needs—at least until he begins showing progress. If your dog is having accidents about every three hours, for instance, the two-and-a-half-hour mark will likely be your ticket to success. A crate can be extremely useful for preventing accidents between trips outdoors, but a wristwatch can be equally helpful. The key is to take him outside before he has a chance to eliminate elsewhere.

In the Doghouse

FAMILY-FRIENDLY TIP

All Hands on Deck

A child can certainly participate in correcting many kinds of canine problem behaviors. If you are trying to stop inappropriate chewing, for example, your kids can play an important part in the solution. Even a preschooler can keep an eye on your pet and alert you if he begins gnawing on an unsuitable object. If you are in the midst of remedial housetraining, your older son or daughter may be able to help by providing your pet with an extra walk after school. If your dog's problem behavior involves biting, though, it is best to limit contact between your pet and your children until a reasonable amount of progress has been made.

Even if you are feeling overwhelmed, it is important that you remain positive and consistent for your pet's sake. If he is only going in the right place every third trip, this is still progress! Reward your dog for each and every success, and keep that routine going even if it feels futile at times. It *will* pay off eventually!

Remember, there is no other mammal with as great a size range as

dogs. In light of this fact, it makes sense that different dogs will need more time between potty breaks than others. For example, the amount of time a Pomchi can wait between trips to empty his tiny bladder will be less than that of a larger dog like a Labradoodle. Keep this in mind as you near the end of your housetraining review. Expecting your dog to hold his bladder and bowels until you can get him to the proper spot is reasonable; asking him to wait hours past his personal limit is not.

Jumping Up

If your dog knows the *sit* and *down* commands, he is well prepared to learn not to jump up. Although you may not care if your dog jumps up on you, people who visit your home or those you encounter while walking your pet may feel differently. Especially if your designer dog is a larger one, he could inadvertently injure a person he is lavishing with attention. The best way to teach him not to jump up as part of his greeting process is to break the habit through practice.

Solution

Your dog's favorite person can be a wonderful helper for this task. Have this "visitor" come to the door and bring your dog to greet her. Before opening the door, instruct your dog to sit. If he stands during his greeting, it's all right as long as he doesn't jump up. If his front legs leave the floor, immediately command him to sit once again. Follow up with the *down* command if you find that he

If your dog is a notorious escape artist, you must have a plan in place to prevent tragedy from striking. It only takes seconds for a dog on the lam to make it to a busy street. Even if he's lucky enough to cross safely, there is nothing to stop him from darting across those lanes again and again—increasing his risk of getting hit by a moving vehicle. Consider implementing a house rule that no exterior doors get opened unless your dog is secured in his kennel or on his leash.

Even with smart safety precautions in place, though, you need to know what to do if your dog breaks loose.

- First, provide your dog with proper identification before he can flee. Microchipping is the most permanent method, but engraved tags with your name, address, and contact information also can be helpful to anyone who encounters your pet.

- Second, spread the word that your dog has run away from home. Phone your neighbors, and enlist the help of friends and family to search for your pet. Post flyers in the windows of any local establishments willing to display them for you.

- Finally, let your veterinarian and local animal shelters know that your pet has been lost.

By acting quickly, you increase your chances of locating your pet tenfold.

Exercise helps this Cockapoo stay physically and mentally healthy.

is too tempted to jump up from the sitting position.

Continue this exercise for between 10 and 15 minutes with your friend repeatedly leaving and coming back through the door. The visitor may speak to your dog or even pat him, as long as he is behaving properly. If he shows too much excitement or jumps up, make sure that your friend discontinues giving attention at once as you redirect your dog. Likewise, make sure that other guests aren't rewarding your dog with attention when he

jumps. Even if they tell you it doesn't bother them, explain politely that it bothers you as you work on correcting the behavior.

You must be careful in praising your dog for complying with your commands in this scenario. While I typically recommend using unabashed verbal praise, you must be careful to constrain your enthusiasm when you reward your dog for not jumping up— your overexcitement could trigger the very problem you are trying to circumvent. This is a case where edible rewards may be an ideal choice.

Separation Anxiety

If your designer dog is excessively howling or barking when he is left alone, this may signal a deeper problem of separation anxiety. If ignored, separation anxiety can further present in the form of chewing, housetraining regression, and sometimes even self-mutilation. One indication that you are dealing with an issue of separation is if you offer your dog a treat when you leave and frequently return to see that it has remained uneaten.

The most common underlying causes of canine separation anxiety are confusion, fear, and stress. A variety of issues could be at the root of the problem. Perhaps your dog was taken from his mother too early, a common occurrence at puppy mills. Maybe your dog's previous owner abandoned him at a shelter, leaving him especially fearful of your leaving him now. Maybe you have returned to working full time after taking a few weeks off to spend with your new puppy. This is a situation in which teaching basic obedience skills can help your dog become a more confident, less anxious being— the key to helping this condition.

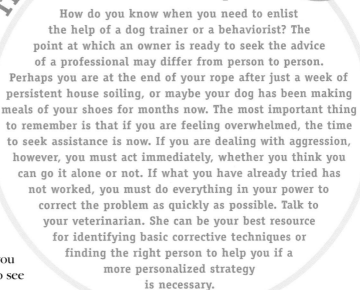

The Expert Knows

Don't Be Afraid to Ask for Help

How do you know when you need to enlist the help of a dog trainer or a behaviorist? The point at which an owner is ready to seek the advice of a professional may differ from person to person. Perhaps you are at the end of your rope after just a week of persistent house soiling, or maybe your dog has been making meals of your shoes for months now. The most important thing to remember is that if you are feeling overwhelmed, the time to seek assistance is now. If you are dealing with aggression, however, you must act immediately, whether you think you can go it alone or not. If what you have already tried has not worked, you must do everything in your power to correct the problem as quickly as possible. Talk to your veterinarian. She can be your best resource for identifying basic corrective techniques or finding the right person to help you if a more personalized strategy is necessary.

Spend time together with your designer dog regularly. Take him for walks often; regular exercise can significantly reduce his stress. Provide your dog with a crate for security, and follow the protocol of slowing introducing it while you are at home. If you cannot seem to correct the problem, consider enrolling your designer dog in daycare or having someone else care of him when you cannot be there. Even having a dog walker stop by midday may offer just enough of a break from the solitude to help your dog cope with being alone while you are away.

Chapter 8

Stepping Out

Owners of designer dogs might worry that without recognition from any major kennel club, they will be limited in the activities available to them and their beloved dogs. Generally, though, this isn't the case. The only event that is truly off-limits to a designer dog is conformation—and even this may not be entirely out of the question.

ertainly, your designer dog won't be receiving any invitations to conformation shows sponsored by the American Kennel Club (AKC) anytime soon, but designer dog clubs (whose growing lists of members include owners just like you) are forming all around the world to celebrate what they love most—their designer dogs.

Sports and Activities

Participating in canine sports is a great way to spend time with your pet while you both reap the added benefits of exercise. Your designer dog doesn't have to possess a near-human talent for playing basketball or soccer like dogs in the movies, though. There are plenty of canine activities tailored specifically to your dog's individual strengths. Many also offer excellent opportunities for socialization.

Agility

If your designer dog has a penchant for playtime, agility may be a fun activity the two of you can share. Requiring speed and dexterity, agility competitions offer dogs a chance to show off their physical prowess. Resembling an equestrian jumping competition, the setting for agility consists of a variety of colorful jumps, vaulted walks, see-saws, A-frames, and tunnels. Handlers lead their dogs through the course by running alongside them and offering either verbal commands or hand signals (or both) as the dogs navigate these obstacles.

Agility can be as fun for spectators as it is for participants, and the sport

It's My Party!

Although designer dogs may never be officially recognized by the AKC—and therefore cannot compete in traditional conformation events—breeders and owners of these increasingly common mixes are beginning to hold less formal specialty events of their own. Labradoodles and Goldendoodles regularly have what they call Doodle Romps, fun-filled gatherings where competitions are held and a great deal of socialization takes place. Ask your breeder if she belongs to a designer dog club that orchestrates get-togethers of this kind, or consider starting your own group. The best way to learn more about a particular designer dog is by spending time with fellow fanciers.

regularly draws impressive crowds. Developed in England in the 1970s, it was first recognized by the AKC in 1994. Unlike the requirements for conformation, a dog need not be purebred to compete in agility, and entrants also may be spayed or neutered. The one requirement that is more stringent, however, is a minimum age of 12 months for all canine participants.

Titles that can be earned in agility are: Novice Agility Dog (NAD), Open Agility Dog (OAD), Agility Dog Excellent (ADX), and Master Agility Excellent (MAX). Not everyone who participates pursues all of these levels, however, or competes in every competition. The best thing about agility is that it is something you can do with your dog right in your own backyard. You need not ever enter a formal competition to participate, though it might be a whole lot of fun!

Canine Good Citizen© Program

One of the best training activities is the completion of the AKC Canine Good Citizen (CGC) program. A certification series begun in 1989, the CGC program stresses responsible pet ownership by rewarding dogs that display good manners both at home and in the community. Those interested may attend the CGC training program, an optional class offered to owners and their dogs, before taking a detailed 10-step test. Upon completion certificates are awarded. All breeds, including designer dogs, are welcome in the program.

The CGC program focuses primarily on a dog's obedience skills and temperament, but it also stresses the importance of serious owner commitment. All owners are required to sign a Responsible Dog Owners Pledge before taking the test. This unique document states that the owner agrees to

effectively care for its dog for the rest of the animal's life. It also encompasses such important areas as health and safety, exercise and training, and basic quality of life. It even addresses such community-based issues as agreeing to clean up after your dog in public and never allowing your dog to infringe on the rights of others.

A dog that passes this valuable examination is awarded an AKC certificate complete with the CGC logo embossed in gold. CGC certification can also be useful to your dog in many other areas of advanced training. A dog worthy of the revered title of Canine Good Citizen is considered a responsible member of his community, a community that includes both people and dogs he

Throwing your dog a party can be a fun activity—this Maltipoo loves celebrating her birthday!

Drink to Your Dog's Health!

Just like people, pets need to prepare their bodies for exercise. A quick warm-up can prevent your dog from pulling muscles or overexerting himself. Before you hit the pavement for that warm-up walk, though, it is wise to visit your vet for a quick checkup to make sure that your dog is up to whatever task you have planned. Finally, safety is not just a before-and-after fitness concern. Keeping your pet hydrated throughout the activity period is also vital, especially in warmer temperatures. Some companies now make sports drinks and bottled water specifically for dogs, but plain old tap water still works just fine for most pets.

already knows and all of those he will encounter in the future.

Although dogs of any age may participate in the CGC program, puppies must be at least old enough to have had all necessary immunizations. To ensure that your dog's certification is reliable, it is strongly recommended that younger dogs that pass the test get re-tested as adults, since temperaments and abilities can possibly change during this formative period.

Obedience

Just as some dogs seem destined for agility, some are amazingly well suited to obedience training. You may notice this when training your dog at home, or this may be your goal from the beginning. Although all purebreds and mixed breeds are welcome to participate in obedience trials, toy-sized dogs certainly have considerably more unchartered territory to explore in this arena than many other canines. Your smaller designer dog is in no way less capable of excelling at obedience, so if you have an interest in this activity, run with it, remembering to heel when appropriate, of course.

Unlike the sport of agility, which focuses on a dog's physical abilities and allows considerable owner interaction, obedience requires more discipline than athleticism; it is truly a test of how well your dog can do on his own. Among the commands your dog will be required to perform at the basic level of competitive obedience are heeling (both on and off his leash), sitting and staying for several minutes at a time, and also standing and staying for similarly fixed time periods. Certainly, owners are involved in every aspect of training (and this is no small task), and they are allowed to issue the commands, but you won't find these owners cheering until the day is done.

Dogs begin competing in the Companion Dog (CD) class and then move on to the Companion Dog Excellent (CDX) class and Utility Dog (UD) class. Ultimately, your designer dog has the potential of earning the highest titles—Obedience Trial Champion (OTCh) and Utility Dog

Excellent (UDX). Both are considered very prestigious accomplishments that are neither easily nor quickly achieved.

Therapy Dogs

If your designer dog has an especially outgoing nature, one of the most enjoyable ways to spend time together may be volunteering at your local hospital or retirement home. The first step is to have your dog certified as a Canine Good Citizen (CGC). Although not mandatory, the AKC offers a CGC training program to owners and their dogs before a ten-step test is administered and certificates are ultimately awarded. Dogs of any age may participate, and yes, crossbreeds are welcome. The test itself focuses on a dog's mastery of basic obedience skills and also his ability to interact peaceably with both human and canine strangers.

Once your dog has attained his CGC status, he is then ready to be evaluated by Therapy Dogs International, Inc., (TDI) an organization formed in 1976 with the goal of bringing caring canines and people in need of their uplifting visits together. Therapy dogs should not be confused with assistance dogs—animals that provide constant one-on-one assistance to people with disabilities. Therapy dogs are considered *emotional service dogs*. Owned privately by people just like you, these dogs have one main goal—to provide joy and comfort to those in need.

Games

Perhaps you discovered your dog's affinity for agility while playing together more informally in your

If your designer dog takes to basic training, you might want to consider participating in obedience events.

Your designer dog might make up his own games to play—these Labradoodles can't resist a little tug of war.

backyard, or maybe you first noticed his aptitude for obedience while teaching him to gently take a cookie from your mouth. Yes, hobbies are often borne of less structured but equally fun pastimes like these. Sometimes, though, playtime is just that—play. This does not mean that leisure time is wasted time. On the contrary, there is often great value in thinking outside the ring, so to speak. By making time for impromptu and creative play, you encourage your dog to show you where his interests and talents truly lie. And you will both undoubtedly have a great time in the process.

There are plenty of informal games you can play with your pet. Most dogs love to play hide and seek. Just be sure your dog is always the seeker. By encouraging him to hide from you, you effectively discourage your dog from

coming to you when called. Conversely, teaching him to seek you out could very possibly save his life one day.

If either you or your dog bore of conventional hide-and-seek, try hiding a favorite toy instead. Many dogs can even be taught to pick up and put away their own toys this way.

Other informal games your designer dog may enjoy playing include tetherball, follow the leader, and even running through the sprinkler on a warm day.

Props also can initiate creative play. I have noticed that my own dogs each seem to have a certain type of toy that inspires them. Molly prefers stuffed animals, whereas Damon prefers braided ropes and balls. Molly likes to play fetch, while Damon enjoys squeaking his playthings. Music also appears to have a lively effect on my dogs. If you've noticed this same reaction in your pet, encourage him to get up and dance with you.

Travel and Vacationing

The decision of whether or not to bring your designer dog on vacation with you can be a tough one. First, you must consider the purpose of the trip. If you are traveling for business and won't have much time to spend with your pet, it may be better to ask a friend to watch your dog or to employ the services of a professional pet sitter. If you are planning a more relaxing getaway, on the other hand, having your precious pet along may only make this time more enjoyable for you both. Many dogs make excellent traveling companions, but there are a few things you can do to stack the odds in your pet's favor before he heads out the doggy door.

By Air

First, gather all of your dog's necessary paperwork. This may include the airline's guidelines for flying with a pet (as well as your dog's tickets) and any health certificates you'll need if you'll be leaving the country. If you are unsure of what is needed, the time to ask questions is well in advance of your departure.

If your designer dog is small enough to fit in a carrier placed under the seat in front of you, chances are good that the airline will allow him to ride in the cabin with you. This is another reason you must make plans beforehand,

A dog-friendly vacation can be fun for the whole family—this Labradoodle loves the beach.

though, because space is sometimes limited. Only so many animals—even small ones—are allowed on each flight. If your designer dog is a larger one, it is highly preferable to plan a road trip than book him a flight in the cargo compartment, the area where bigger pets are remanded. While this section of the plane is fine for luggage, the extreme temperatures and loud noises make it a very unfriendly place for pets.

By Car

Always remember that safety comes first when traveling by car, so keep your dog securely in his crate while riding. A canine safety belt can be used for shorter trips around town, but unlike this more restrictive device, a crate will allow your dog to change position and move around a bit during the trip. Remember to make frequent stops so that your dog can relieve his bladder and bowels, and always give him a drink before heading back out on the road. Also, never leave your dog unattended in your vehicle.

Feed your dog only a light meal prior to the trip—never immediately before leaving the house. This can help to prevent stomach upset. If your dog tends to get nauseous when riding, however, feeding him a few ginger snaps may help, since ginger has been shown to prevent motion sickness in dogs.

What to Pack

When traveling, space is usually an unavoidable consideration, but safety should always determine which items top your pet's packing list. Fortunately, most of these must-haves are small.

SENIOR DOG TIP

Let Him Ride

You may worry that the stress of travel might be too much for your older dog. If so, consider how he may feel if left at home instead. Perhaps you have never boarded your dog. If not, the hectic nature of travel may pale in comparison to the anxiety your dog may feel from being in this unfamiliar environment until you return. There are several steps you can take to make him more comfortable while he accompanies you on your road trip. These include making frequent stops for him to stretch his legs and relieve his bladder and bringing along a cushiony liner for his crate, the safest car seat for your pet. If you will be flying and your larger designer dog cannot accompany you in the airplane's cabin, it may actually be better for him to skip the trip. Instead, consider asking a friend to pet sit (or hiring a professional) instead of boarding your dog so that he can remain in the comfort of his own home until you return.

Designer Dogs

First, always be sure that your pet is affixed with at least one form of identification. Even if your dog has been microchipped, adding a more obvious ID tag to his collar is a smart and inexpensive step. Your dog also should be properly restrained while riding in your vehicle, so either bring along a crate or secure him with a canine safety belt. Fresh water should always be within your reach. Waiting to fill your dog's thermos until you reach the next rest stop is impractical. Instead, use your refueling stops as opportunities to refill this

This Maltipoo never travels anywhere without a fashionable jacket!

container. Other important items to stash in your pet's bag include food, a canine first-aid kit, your dog's leash and collar, a towel or blanket, baby wipes, zip-style plastic bags, and toys. Although toys might not be an absolute necessity, they can keep your pet entertained during a long drive. This translates to a more relaxing trip for everyone.

Whether you are at home or on the road, the most important thing is that you make time to spend with your dog regularly. What you choose to do together actually matters very little. Whether your designer dog is a Labradoodle, Pomchi, or any other combination, what he needs most is your time and love, truly the best combination of all.

FAMILY-FRIENDLY TIP

Toy With Them

Whether you are traveling with dogs, kids, or both, one of the best ways to make a trip a peaceful one is by bringing along plenty of toys—the more interactive the better. The goal is to keep everyone entertained. Limit the number of noisy playthings, and be sure to rotate items to avoid boredom. Like books and video games for children, nylon bones and hollow toys that dispense treats can make the ride a bit more bearable for your canine kid.

Resources

Associations and Organizations

Breed Clubs
American Canine Hybrid Club
10509 S & G Circle
Harvey, AR 72841
Telephone: (479) 299-4415
www.achclub.com

Pet Sitters
National Association of Professional Pet Sitters
15000 Commerce Parkway, Suite C
Mt. Laurel, New Jersey 08054
Telephone: (856) 439-0324
Fax: (856) 439-0525
E-mail: napps@ahint.com
www.petsitters.org

Pet Sitters International
201 East King Street
King, NC 27021-9161
Telephone: (336) 983-9222
Fax: (336) 983-5266
E-mail: info@petsit.com
www.petsit.com

Rescue Organizations and Animal Welfare Groups
American Humane Association (AHA)
63 Inverness Drive East
Englewood, CO 80112
Telephone: (303) 792-9900
Fax: 792-5333
www.americanhumane.org

American Society for the Prevention of Cruelty to Animals (ASPCA)
424 E. 92nd Street
New York, NY 10128-6804
Telephone: (212) 876-7700
www.aspca.org

Royal Society for the Prevention of Cruelty to Animals (RSPCA)
Telephone: 0870 3335 999
Fax: 0870 7530 284
www.rspca.org.uk

The Humane Society of the United States (HSUS)
2100 L Street, NW
Washington DC 20037
Telephone: (202) 452-1100
www.hsus.org

Therapy
Delta Society
875 124th Ave NE, Suite 101
Bellevue, WA 98005
Telephone: (425) 226-7357
Fax: (425) 235-1076
E-mail: info@deltasociety.org
www.deltasociety.org

Therapy Dogs Incorporated
PO Box 5868
Cheyenne, WY 82003
Telephone: (877) 843-7364
E-mail: therdog@sisna.com
www.therapydogs.com

Therapy Dogs International (TDI)
88 Bartley Road
Flanders, NJ 07836
Telephone: (973) 252-9800
Fax: (973) 252-7171
E-mail: tdi@gti.net
www.tdi-dog.org

Training
Association of Pet Dog Trainers (APDT)
150 Executive Center Drive Box 35
Greenville, SC 29615
Telephone: (800) PET-DOGS
Fax: (864) 331-0767
E-mail: information@apdt.com
www.apdt.com

Veterinary and Health Resources

Academy of Veterinary Homeopathy (AVH)
P.O. Box 9280
Wilmington, DE 19809
Telephone: (866) 652-1590
Fax: (866) 652-1590
E-mail: office@TheAVH.org
www.theavh.org

American Academy of Veterinary Acupuncture (AAVA)
100 Roscommon Drive, Suite 320
Middletown, CT 06457
Telephone: (860) 635-6300
Fax: (860) 635-6400
E-mail: office@aava.org
www.aava.org

American Animal Hospital Association (AAHA)
P.O. Box 150899
Denver, CO 80215-0899
Telephone: (303) 986-2800
Fax: (303) 986-1700
E-mail: info@aahanet.org
www.aahanet.org/index.cfm

American College of Veterinary Internal Medicine (ACVIM)
1997 Wadsworth Blvd., Suite A
Lakewood, CO 80214-5293
Telephone: (800) 245-9081
Fax: (303) 231-0880
Email: ACVIM@ACVIM.org
www.acvim.org

American College of Veterinary Ophthalmologists (ACVO)
P.O. Box 1311
Meridian, Idaho 83860
Telephone: (208) 466-7624
Fax: (208) 466-7693
E-mail: office@acvo.com
www.acvo.com

American Holistic Veterinary Medical Association (AHVMA)
2218 Old Emmorton Road
Bel Air, MD 21015
Telephone: (410) 569-0795

Fax: (410) 569-2346
E-mail: office@ahvma.org
www.ahvma.org

American Veterinary Medical Association (AVMA)
1931 North Meacham Road – Suite 100
Schaumburg, IL 60173
Telephone: (847) 925-8070
Fax: (847) 925-1329
E-mail: avmainfo@avma.org
www.avma.org

ASPCA Animal Poison Control Center
1717 South Philo Road, Suite 36
Urbana, IL 61802
Telephone: (888) 426-4435
www.aspca.org

British Veterinary Association (BVA)
7 Mansfield Street
London
W1G 9NQ
Telephone: 020 7636 6541
Fax: 020 7436 2970
E-mail: bvahq@bva.co.uk
www.bva.co.uk

Canine Eye Registration Foundation (CERF)
VMDB/CERF
1248 Lynn Hall
625 Harrison St.
Purdue University
West Lafayette, IN 47907-2026
Telephone: (765) 494-8179
E-mail: CERF@vmbd.org
www.vmdb.org

Orthopedic Foundation for Animals (OFA)
2300 NE Nifong Blvd
Columbus, Missouri 65201-3856
Telephone: (573) 442-0418
Fax: (573) 875-5073
Email: ofa@offa.org
www.offa.org

Index

111

Dedication

This book is dedicated to all the designer dogs, purebreds, and mutts of the world. Each and every one of you is special in your own right.

Acknowledgements

I would like to thank the following breeders for speaking with me about their experiences with designer dogs: Debbie Bruce, Kelly Corbeil, Tanya Dvorak, Sherri and Roger Halvorson, Christina Long, Terry Raposa, Jodi Russell, Ed and Tersea Schwalbach, and Nancy Smallwood.

About the Author

Tammy Gagne is a freelance writer who specializes in the health and behavior of companion animals. She is a regular contributor to several national pet care magazines and has owned purebred dogs for more than 25 years. In addition to being an avid dog lover, she is also an experienced aviculturist. She resides in northern New England with her husband, son, dogs, and parrots.